From Victim to VICTOR

How to Rise from Paralyzing Fear and Crippling Beliefs to Soar into Empowered Freedom

Jennifer Hoffman

FROM VICTIM TO VICTOR

Published by Feed Your Muse Press, LLC, A division of Enlightening Life OmniMedia, Inc.

Visit our website at www.enlighteninglife.com

ISBN 13 978-0-9821949-5-9

ISBN 10 0-9821949-5-1

The information provided in this book is designed to provide helpful information on the subjects discussed. This book is not meant to be used, nor should it be used, to diagnose or treat any medical or mental health condition. For diagnosis or treatment of any medical problem, consult your own physician. The publisher and author are not responsible for any specific health or other needs that may require medical supervision and are not liable for any damages or negative consequences from any treatment, action, application or preparation, to any person reading or following the information in this book. References are provided for informational purposes only and do not constitute endorsement of any websites or other sources. Readers should be aware that any websites referred to in this book may change.

Dedication

To the little girl who was determined to walk

and learned to soar

Once she changed her victim thinking

So she could find her wings.

And to everyone who has a dream in their heart,

so they can rise above defeat, determined to

overcome their paralysis and crippling fear,

healing the victim they think they are

to become the victor who

embraces life with radiant confidence and joy.

ther titles by Jennifer Hoffman

) Days to Everyday Miracles

scending into Miracles – The Path of Spiritual Mastery

he Atlantis Legacy -- Taking Humanity Through 2012 and Beyond

he Human Energy Control Protocols – the Secret Agenda to Control Your nergy and Rule the World

isit www.enlighteninglife.com to learn more about Jennifer's books, CDs, ›aching, personal sessions and other services.

Table of Contents

Everyone Has a Victim Story

Do you think you're a victim? Don't be afraid to say 'yes' because everyone has had at least one life experience (and more often several of them) which caused them to feel like a victim.

Do any of these represent your victim story?

You were bullied some point in your life

Someone has physically, mentally, emotionally, or spiritually abused you

You have experienced a major physical or emotional life trauma

A friend or significant partner has hurt or betrayed you

At some point in your life you have not felt loved or valued enough

You have had an experience of being unable to control life events or circumstances

You have suffered a devastating loss or disappointment at some point in your life.

Or, like me, something happened to you (you'll read about my victim story in a minute) that you could not control for a variety of reasons, and your life changed in the space of a moment. Then you had to focus all of your energy on surviving the situation and to chose whether you would learn how to overcome it or forever be a victim of its effects.

Any incident, no matter how big or small, has the potential to make you feel powerless, paralyzed, crippled, unworthy, incapable, afraid of expressing yourself, going after your dreams, or attempting to achieve your goals.

It is true -- any life situation has the potential to defeat you, to make you believe and think that you are a victim. But you get to choose whether or not you interpret these experiences in that way, and then become and remain a victim of them. Once you have had one of these potentially victimizing experiences, it is permanently imprinted in your mind and a lot of limiting beliefs are created around it, although you can rise above it and I'll show you how that could be possible for you.

Have you ever had thoughts like:

I will never be able to do that.

I can't imagine that this will work out for me.

I won't ever let that happen to me again.

I'm trying to succeed but it just isn't working for me.

My life is a mess and I'll never be able to change it.

I should be able to get over this and move on but I just can't do it.

I am not good enough to succeed.

These are powerful words and if you say even one of those sentences to yourself, what you say, think, or affirm is being created in your life every time you say or think it. Everything that we think and say is immediately reflected in our life. Without exception.

What are you creating in your life today? Success, happiness, prosperity, and abundance?

Or unhappiness, poor health, bad relationships, and financial lack?

Think about it. What if your every thought became a tangible, visible thing, appearing in front of you?

How would you feel about them?

Would you be proud of your now visible thoughts that you and everyone around you could see, or would you be ashamed of your thoughts and try to hide them from others, including yourself?

Are your thoughts and words reinforcing your beliefs that you are a victim, afraid, confused, wounded, crippled, and powerless, or are you proclaiming that you are a victor who is fearless, confident, healed, whole, and powerful?

If you knew that you could change everything in your life that you feel is not working for you or that is not giving you the results or life outcomes you want, and create a life in which you were happy, successful, financially secure, and fulfilled in every way, doing exactly what you wanted to do, every day, would you be willing to try it?

What if I told you that it would take absolutely no physical effort and involved just changing a few simple words that you use every day and turning some existing beliefs around to move from victim to victor?

Would you try it then or would you even believe that it was possible for you to stop being a victim in your life?

If you answered 'yes' to the questions above then you're ready for a change. So, are you willing to go one step farther to be determined to overcome what has been crippling your dreams, no matter how long you have been living with it, and become a more confident, powerful version of yourself, instead of being a victim?

All it takes is your willingness to do that -- but nothing can happen unless you're willing to take that first step.

This book is a journey that will take you from where you are, living through your victim story and crippled by your life's past events that paralyze you with fear and doubt, to where you want to be, from victim consciousness to victorious mastery, from being crippled by your painful memories to being proud, confident, and clear, moving you from paralysis to power, from being a victim to becoming a victor.

Maybe you have never thought that you could create a life you love and fulfill your dreams. But you can. Everyone can. All it takes is an awareness of how you got to where you are today and a willingness to change how you think and talk, along with a desire to do things differently. No kidding.

I'm going to start by sharing my story with you, the story of how I went from being physically paralyzed when I was five years old, unable to move a muscle, told by doctors that I would never walk again (and refusing to believe it), to confidently walking, running, riding a bike, and doing things that I was never supposed to be able to do.

The only thing I could not do was become a ballet dancer, which was my dream. Being paralyzed for so many years and the resulting muscle and nerve damage rendered that that impossible. But I can do other things and do them very well, which I'll share with you so you can see how while there are things that your victim experiences may prevent you from doing, you can focus on mastering other things.

And I'll talk about how I became a victim of my experiences and allowed them to cripple my life in many ways, until they became the limitations I created my life with and through.

One day, I learned how to transform my victim consciousness and became a victor. You can do this too when you are tired of being a victim and want to live your life in another way.

Then we'll talk about your victim story, your paralysis and how it cripples you, and how it all started, beginning with what happened in your life to create your victim beliefs.

Your beliefs, perceptions, and attitudes play a critical role in the life you create for yourself -- you will learn how to identify the ones that are holding you back from achieving the prosperity, success, joy, and happiness that you deserve and change them so that you can create the life that you want and are happy with.

Negative words create negative situations in your life. I call them 'crippling' words because they prevent you from moving forward. It's not a word that is used very often today, but it means to be 'impaired' or 'disabled'. In this state you cannot function optimally, at your full potential, that's why I use that word in this way. It's also what people used to call me, 'crippled', at a time in my life when I was physically disabled, so it's a word that has a lot of meaning for me.

You will learn what these 'crippling' words are, which ones to avoid, and how to change the way you speak so that every word you use creates the possibility for prosperity, the right kind of abundance, success, and happiness in your life.

The Universal Law of Energy says that everything is energy, including you, and everything you think or talk about is manifested in your life (it has to be, because it is energy). This Law also says that energy attracts similar energy and we cannot attract an energy that is higher than our own energy at any moment. You will learn how to make this Universal Law work for you in the best possible ways, so that you are using your energy to create and attract positive opportunities for prosperity, success, wealth, and happiness.

You will learn how to create the life that you are happy with and proud to live, a life full of success, prosperity, wealth, and joy that is possible as long as you actively create it, believe it, and act upon it. You can stop being a victim and become a victor.

It's a fascinating journey that will change your life...But before we take that first step, let me tell you about a paralyzed little girl who became a crippled adult until she learned how to stop being a victim of her life experiences...

From Paralyzed to Powerful

It was late in the afternoon on a beautiful autumn day and I was playing outside. At the time I was five years old and had just entered kindergarten. Inspired by the little ballerina in a pink tutu who turned a pirouette every time I lifted the lid of my little jewelry box, I wanted to be a ballet dancer and was going to start ballet lessons soon.

That afternoon, though, my mind was on other things. My sister had a red tricycle which she never let me ride and there it was, on the sidewalk in front of me, and she was not around. I ran towards it, hoping to ride it for a few minutes before she returned to claim it.

But before I reached it I fell down and hurt my leg. Someone ran to get my mother, who carried me home, where she saw I had a deep gash in my left knee that was going to require stitches, so we went to the emergency room. The doctor also gave me a DPT (diphtheria polio tetanus) vaccine after my knee was stitched up.

Several days later I didn't feel well at school and my parents came to take me home. I soon developed a very high fever and I couldn't move, so my parents took me to the hospital again. The last thing I remember was lying in the back seat of the car, staring out the back window and seeing the stars in the night sky.

I awakened from a coma a week later, lying in a bed in a hospital room and saw my parents standing by the door, talking to a doctor. I thought it was strange that I could not feel any part of my body except my head. In a short while I learned that I had been paralyzed from the neck down by a condition called Guillain Barre Syndrome, an auto-immune disease which causes the body to attack the central nervous system, and it is caused by a negative reaction to vaccines. It was how my body responded to the DPT vaccine I had received the week before, when the gash in my knee was stitched up. Although doctors were optimistic that I had not suffered brain damage from the high fever and coma, they were not sure that I would ever walk again.

And that is the conversation I overheard between my parents and the doctor when I regained consciousness from the coma. At the time, this was in 1963, doctors didn't think about children hearing and understanding conversations, especially young children. But when I heard the doctor tell my parents "Jennifer will probably never walk again", I thought to myself "Oh yes I will", and I did, although it would take another five years for me to accomplish that.

My hospital stay stretched into months as I slowly began to regain the use of my arms and legs. My physical therapy included painful leg and arm exercises, and to regain the use of my hands, I learned how to braid. At this point I really felt like a victim — I had a brother and a sister, why was I the one who was sick? I couldn't play outside or move like other kids, why had this happened to me? I missed my family and missed being at home.

Why had this happened to me? The victim thinking had begun. I was struggling with being paralyzed and in the hospital, but I also wondered why this had happened to me and not someone else. How had I become so unlucky? What had I done to deserve this?

One of the worst parts of my physical therapy was the body cast. To prevent my muscles from atrophying, since they were not being used properly, I had to sleep in a body cast at night, which straightened and stretched my arms and legs. A new cast had to be created every two weeks, since I was very young and was still growing.

To create the cast, my body was wrapped from the neck down in large sheets of cotton wool (this is how it was done in the 1960s), which was then covered with wet plaster bandages. The nurses tried to minimize the discomfort by soaking the bandages in warm water but it was still a very uncomfortable process. I could not be moved while the plaster dried, which included using the toilet or bedpan.

The cast was cut off of my body with a small rotary saw which burned me if they accidentally touched my skin with it, which they did occasionally, despite doing their best not to. Then an inch was trimmed off of the arms and legs of the cast and they were put back together. Every night I was laid face up in the body cast, which looked like a sarcophagus, my arms and legs were straightened and stretched, the cast was closed and I laid there all night, by myself. I cried a lot at night because the cast was uncomfortable and when I began to regain sensation in my feet, it tickled my heels.

Over time I slowly regained feeling and movement, graduated from being confined to a bed, then a wheelchair, then walking with hip to ankle leg braces and crutches, then short leg braces without crutches. I had to wear ugly brown orthopedic shoes, which my leg braces were attached to. Going anywhere was a struggle and I always felt like such an inconvenience to my family. But even worse than that, wherever I went, people stared at me and whispered, "What's wrong with her?".

By the time I was eleven years old I could walk unassisted and do everything like most children, with some limitations because I lost part of my sense of balance and my right leg didn't return to its full strength. One of my Christmas presents that year was a shiny blue 'Sting Ray' bicycle with a glittery blue banana seat, white basket, and long sparkly blue fringe at the ends of the big, curved handle bars. I loved that bicycle, not just because it was fashionable, but because being able to ride it was a victory for me and meant that I had recovered from the paralysis.

But while my physical body recovered from its paralysis, it was still present in hidden ways. I developed a fear that something terrible would happen to me if I went after what I wanted (my parents associated my knee injury from falling while running to ride the tricycle with the paralysis), I did not want to do anything to inconvenience them and always felt like I was 'in the way' (having a handicapped child in the 1960s was not easy for them). And after years of being stared at and whispered about, I developed a very strong fear of being the one who was 'different', the center of attention, or of being shamed.

My parents always reminded me of how "I almost died" and although I did have a near death experience when I was in a coma during the first week of my illness, I developed a very strong fear of death and dying. I wasn't really afraid of dying, I was afraid that if I took any kind of risk, that something bad would happen to me and I may die or worse, be paralyzed again. Or I would be an inconvenience to my parents again, and complicate their lives.

It took many years for me to understand that although I had overcome the paralysis, I was still a 'cripple' in many ways and I had developed a victim story around my illness. While my body recovered, in my mind I saw myself as a victim, who was once crippled by something I could not control, and had a constant fear that it would happen again. This victim story crippled my dreams for many years, preventing me from pursuing what I wanted, limiting my options to things that were safe or not risky, and compelling me to unconsciously sabotage anything that came too close to the achievement of real success, until I could identify this pattern and learned how to transform my beliefs, overcoming the victim to become a victor. What I learned in that process is what I am going to share with you.

The source of your paralysis doesn't matter, whether it is from a bad relationship, terrible childhood, any kind of abuse, an injury, a job loss, rejection, betrayal, poor self worth, sadness, or depression – the list of paralyzing factors is very long.

It doesn't matter if it happened one time or many times. What does matter is that these situations continue to cripple you until you release your victim thinking and let go of your victim story. Until you do, it repeats itself, creating many opportunities for you to experience your victimhood again and again, until you can release it and see yourself as a victor. Then you can create your life in positive, self affirming ways that bring you freedom and joy.

Are you beginning to see a victim story or theme in your life? Are you ready to take the first steps towards transformation? Let's take one of those first steps now… and see what it means to be a victim.

The Victim Within

Do you feel like a victim in your own life or of life in general?
Do bad things always seem to happen to you?
Do you never get ahead, no matter how hard you try?
Do you think that you were born under an unlucky star because nothing in your life ever goes right?
Do you think that all of the lucky breaks in the world are enjoyed by everyone else?

If that's how you feel about your life, then you are a victim. And do you know what? You may continue to be a victim for the rest of your life. Because that's what you believe and that is what your beliefs will create in your life. Nothing more. In fact, as long as you believe this, nothing in your life will ever change.

You will get the same kind of life, every day, day in and day out, week after week, month after month, and year after year.

I remember a time in my life when things were going extremely badly and every day a new disaster would bring more drama into my life. Everything was going wrong and my life was a mess. This was long before I was aware of how my childhood paralysis had crippled my thinking, created my victim mindset, and set me on the path of believing that I would never be able to control my life. Within the first ten minutes of a conversation, the person I was talking to knew about my five most recent disasters and how hard my life was.

It's a little embarrassing, when I think back on those days, to remember how I unloaded my victim dramas on everyone I met. It was so easy it was for me to share my victim story and spread my bad tidings to get pity and sympathy. What I didn't know was that until I stopped talking about my victim story nothing was ever going to change and I would continue to have never-ending drama that made me feel even more like a victim and that I was creating it because I believed I was a victim.

I was in the middle of a very long, hard, victim cycle and it would take years for me to escape from it. The only people in my life were those whose lives were as bad as or worse than mine was. Everyone else stayed away from me, probably because they were afraid that my bad luck would rub off on them.

Now I'm not trivializing your life experiences and you may have many reasons to feel like a victim. But beyond the events which contributed to your victim thinking or set you on that path, being a victim is created through your beliefs and once you ***believe*** that you are a victim, victimhood becomes your mindset. You probably tell everyone you know and a few people that you do not know, about how bad your life is, its terrible circumstances, and how nothing goes right for you.

Each new conversation becomes another opportunity to share your misery. And each new disaster becomes another confirmation of your victimhood. And these people probably agree with you and are sympathetic, because their lives are in a terrible state as well. In fact, they are probably victims too.

Victims are attracted to victims, and if they weren't victims, they would not be in your circle of friends.

What does that mean? Let me explain. Are you familiar with the saying 'Misery loves company'? Have you noticed that people who are down and out always seem to be attracted to each other? They get together and talk about their misery, their problems, their bad luck, and their failures. In essence, they feed on each other's pain and they find power in their shared misery.

If you have friends or acquaintances like this, you know that being with them can make you feel better because you can always find someone who has more problems than you do. Or someone who is worse off than you are. And that makes you feel better. Yes, your life is bad but your friend Joe's life is even worse. That gives you some relief and lets you believe that your life isn't so bad.

But what this does is create even more misery in your life because you don't have any reason or impetus to change your situation. All you do is talk about the unhappy state of your life, which ensures that you remain a victim. And, as long as you continue to mingle with people who are just as or even more victimized by life than you are, you will continue to reaffirm the fact that you are a victim and hey, you're doing OK, because it could be even worse. You know that because you are always around people who have it just as bad as or much worse than you do.

There is another principle at work here and it is called the Law of Attraction. The Law of Attraction states that you attract everything that you think, believe, and talk about to your life. So, if you think and talk about how bad your life is, you get more of the same.

If you think and talk about how unhappy, broke, angry, sick, tired, upset, and frustrated you are, that's exactly what you get.

But, you're saying, that *is* what is going on in my life right now so what else can I talk about?

At this moment, you may not be able to think of anything else to talk about but your problems, but as long as you continue to talk and think about them and affirm their presence in your life, you will only receive more problems.

Thinking and talking about your misery and pain does not improve your situation, even if it makes you feel better when you share your misery with others who can sympathize with you.

You have to introduce new energy into your life to create change. So to stop being a victim you have to stop hanging around with people who are victims and to stop thinking, talking, and acting like a victim.

Let me ask you another question. Do you have any friends who are not victims, people whose lives are going great, who are happy, successful, and rich? Probably not. Why? Because they are not victims and they are not attracted to your victim status. When you are a victim, it manifests not only in your life's circumstances, it is also reflected in everything about you and around you. The way you walk, talk and act all tell everyone around you that are a victim.

You might as well have a big 'VICTIM' sign pasted on your forehead.

You may not even be aware of it, but if you feel like a victim, then you walk like a victim and talk like a victim. And you act like a victim. Why? Because what we have within us is reflected to the outside world. It is the Universal Law of Correspondence, "As within, so without."

Therefore, people who are not victims will avoid you because you do not have anything to offer them that they want or can connect with, and they will see that big **VICTIM** sign that's flashing on your forehead from a mile away.

They won't want to hear about your problems and your misery and they won't have any misery or problems to share with you. In fact, being around them would only make you feel worse because it would only highlight the fact that your life is a mess, compared to theirs. And being around you makes them feel uncomfortable because all you can focus on is your problems and they focus on other things, like their prosperity, success, and happiness.

But, you need to be around people who are not victims because they would provide you with an opportunity to focus on something other than what's wrong with your life, to help you to find things that are 'right' with your life, and become your example of what is possible once you release your victim thinking.

So what do you do?

That's what we're going to focus on. We will first discuss how you became a victim, the power of beliefs and perceptions, what a victor is, the difference between a victim and a victor, the power of the words 'I AM' and how you can change from being a victim to being a VICTOR. Your ultimate goal is to have R - E – S – P – E – C – T for yourself and from others. It's easy, it doesn't cost anything other than how much you value being a victim, and anyone can do it.

That doesn't mean that whatever created your victim story will go away. You'll still have the reminders of it, whether they are physical, mental, emotional, or spiritual. I have a lasting reminder of my paralysis and its victim story because I walk with a slight limp that gets worse when I am tired or have been walking too much. My right leg retained permanent muscle and nerve damage which can be painful at times (another side effect of Guillain Barre Syndrome) and it has never fully recovered from its paralysis. So I don't have to tell anyone about my victim story because it shows in the way I walk.

And people notice it and ask me 'what's wrong with my leg'. Every time I hear that, I am taken back to decades ago, when people would ask my parents what was wrong with me, or they stared at me, or avoided me out of embarrassment or fear. For years I felt different, imperfect, and wrong because I wasn't like everyone else. I could walk and get around like other people, but I felt like I was still wearing the ugly brown orthopedic shoes and uncomfortable braces on my legs.

And because I felt imperfect, people who were also operating at less than their full potential were drawn to me and I had a lot of victim friends. I believed that people who were more 'perfect' wouldn't want to hang around with me, so I did my best to stay away from them.

It's pretty sad when I realize how long I lived my life that way. And you are probably living that way too, if you are allowing a life trauma of any kind that once paralyzed you with fear to now cripple you with a lack of confidence, belief in your imperfection, and a sense of unworthiness.

You're ready for a change, to do something different. You're ready to move from paralysis to being powerful, from crippling doubt and indecision to being confidently creative, from defeat to determination. Here's one way to start right now by affirming to yourself …

I AM A VICTOR!

Being a Victim

If you're a victim, you know it and it is reflected in every part of your life. You probably do not feel very successful and you're not even close to meeting your goals. In fact, you may not even have any goals anymore because you have never been able to meet them in the past, so why bother thinking about them now.

Why would you do anything that would eventually set you up to fail again, so you would feel even more unhappy or depressed than you are now, when nothing works out for you anyway? And you know that whatever you want to do is not going to work out because it never has before.

If you're a victim, you feel that life dealt you a terrible hand. When life handed you lemons, you did your best to make lemonade, but someone hid the sugar bowl from you and all you can make is very tart, lemon-flavored water.

If you're a victim, nothing in your life is going well--you hate your job, your house, your relationships, and maybe even your friends. You don't get along with your neighbors or your family and you are not very happy with your life or with yourself.

If you have a business, it probably is not doing too well either and you may be struggling or barely scraping by. You wonder when you are going to get fired or laid off from your job and when that happens, you don't know how you are ever going to find another one.

If you're a victim, nothing you try works the way you want it to. In fact, you may have quit trying to figure out how things, including your life, will work out because it's probably going to all turn out just as it has in the past. Right?

You probably don't have any money, either, and you're not even close to living the life of your dreams.

Do you have any dreams, goals or ambitions? Probably not, because they will just turn out to be another disappointment. Every time you try something new or do something different, the rug gets pulled out from under you and you're right back where you started.

If you're single, you only meet jerks or people you would not dream of introducing to your friends or your family.

If you're married, your marriage may be hanging on by a thread and the only reason you don't leave your wife or your husband is that you can't afford to or you're afraid to be alone. Maybe your wife or husband has left you and you are alone, feeling rejected, dejected, and angry. Even if you did try to meet someone new, the next person would probably treat you just as badly as the person you were just with.

If you have children, they are probably giving you as many headaches and heartaches as everything else in your life does.

Does this describe your life?

When did you become a victim? It may have been part of your development process during childhood, based on your experiences and the interaction between you and your parents. It may have started in school or when you reached adulthood, after several failed jobs, relationships, marriages, or other dreams that you could never achieve.

You may have been abused or mistreated by someone at some point in your life. Or you may, like me, have experienced a traumatic life event that spiraled out of control and created very permanent consequences. As I said, I still walk with a slight limp and I always will; it is a permanent reminder of my paralysis.

There are many reasons for the development of a victim consciousness. And there are just as many ways to overcome it.

Now you're probably asking yourself "Is there any way to turn this around?"

Is my life ever going to get any better?

How did I get this way?

What did I do to deserve this?

Why me?

The good news is that you can change all of these circumstances and the fact that you are reading this book means that you are ready for a change. All of those questions will be answered and you will discover how to stop being a victim and become a victor.

To discover how you got this way and what is creating this situation in your life, we'll have to look at your beliefs and perceptions. So we're going to take a trip back to the past, to your childhood, where your victim beliefs and perceptions, which paralyzed, crippled, and defeated you, were developed...

The Power of Beliefs and Perceptions

When you were born you started life with unlimited possibilities for success. You were a blank page, ready to receive and remember all of the information that you needed for growth and survival. Think about little babies for a minute. Only three things are important in a baby's life, security, control, and approval. The person who takes care of them when they need to be held, fed, and diapered is meeting their security needs. Their control needs are met by knowing that they can cry when they need something and someone will be there to care for them. The loving attention they get from their mother or father or the people who care for them meets their approval needs. When a baby cries or laughs and coos and receives smiles and loving care, they receive the approval they need and they are happy.

So, what happens when those needs are not met? If any **one** of those needs is not met, the baby develops the belief that something in their environment is dangerous or harmful to their survival and they are on their way to becoming a victim. This is a very important time in a person's life because it is when their belief systems begin to develop. If any of a young baby's security, control, and approval needs are not met, they begin to believe that the world is a big, bad place with no one to protect them and provide them with the security, control, and approval that they need.

They then develop the belief systems that will support those opinions. Depending on how severe this is, the long-term effects can range from mild to severe, from some anxiety to a full blown lack of confidence and a general fear of the world.

Now fast forward through childhood, as that baby grows up and approaches its teenage years. Chances are that parents who did not respond to the baby's security, control, and approval needs are having their own problems and are not able to provide those things to the child as it continues to grow and develop. And all of the unmet security, control, and approval needs are taking the child farther down the path of victimhood.

A short clarification here: children don't have a concept of time and they have not yet developed the experience that provides them with an ability to compare situations. So, something that happens to them once might as well have happened one hundred times. In their minds, one time is all it takes to cement a belief firmly in place. Ask anyone around you to remember a difficult or painful childhood situation or something they were told in their childhood that they still remember and they will come up with at least one or more examples and describe them as though they happened in the last twenty-four hours.

Here's an example of that from one of my childhood memories. When I was three years old someone gave me a little jewelry set with a necklace and a ring. Of course, I wore them all day and at bedtime I insisted on wearing them to bed. My grandmother told me that if I wore a necklace to bed it would wrap itself around my neck and choke me when I slept and the ring would come off of my finger, get into my mouth, and get stuck in my throat, choking me. I now know she told me that because she didn't want me to wear the necklace and ring to bed. But I didn't know that then and since I loved and trusted my grandmother (she was my favorite relative), I believed her implicitly.

Since that day (and this was a one-time incident), I have never, ever worn any kind of jewelry to bed. Would I get choked in my sleep by a necklace? Would a ring come off of my finger and somehow get stuck in my throat while I was sleeping? Probably not, but I would not consider wearing one to find out. Although I'm much older now, I remember every detail of that discussion, including my fear, as though it happened yester-day. And I still remove all of my jewelry before going to bed.

Children are like sponges--they absorb everything that they see and hear and they remember everything in great detail. They form their beliefs and perceptions about life in general and about how life will treat them from what they experience and everything they are told. They also form strong beliefs based on their experiences. A parent who doesn't meet their security, control, and approval needs creates the belief that the world will not provide for them, that they aren't worthy of being loved, supported, and cared for, and that no one will respond to their needs. Their paralyzing situation has been created, and the victim beliefs that will cripple them have been fixed in place and will be reinforced by their life experiences.

But this is learned behavior because the parents are merely reflect-ing their own victim beliefs to their children. When the parents' security, control, and approval needs are not being met, they send strong verbal and non-verbal messages to their children, as well as not meeting the children's security, control and approval needs.

Do you see where this is heading?

Parents with a victim story and victim consciousness often say things like 'I never get a break,' or 'life is terrible,' or 'I'm always getting taken advantage of by my boss,' or 'I never have any money.'

Parents who are overly critical, overly permissive, who constantly judge their children, who create situations where their children feel unloved or unwanted, or who set unreasonable expectations of them, are also not meeting their children's security, control, and approval needs.

Children listen to and absorb everything they hear their parents say. Then, they watch and remember everything that their parents do, and that creates additional beliefs. If parents talk about how hard life is, how they can't get ahead, how they hate their jobs, how difficult their relationships are, how they just can't seem to make ends meet, or get what they want, in front of their children, they are passing along their victim consciousness to them and a new generation of victims is created.

Their children will develop similar victim belief systems because that's all they have ever heard, all of their life, from their parents, family, and from their parents' friends. And since they want to make their parents happy and to be just like them, they will automatically mimic their parents' victim behavior, speech, and thoughts.

Is it surprising that these children will become victims, partner with other victims, and create victim lifestyles? Remember, misery loves company and victims are always attracted to other victims.

From these beliefs, then, children develop their perceptions about how the world is going to treat them and make decisions about their chances for success in the world. They begin to perceive the world as being a cold, angry, and mean place that doesn't and won't meet their needs because it didn't meet their parents' needs. They have proof of that because their parents are the central authority in life, as far as they are concerned. And that is what they have heard their parents say.

If their parents can't make it or succeed, how can they?

If their parents are victims, they will become victims too.

If the parents are paralyzed by their own fears, doubts, and events that have crippled them in their lives, they pass that paralysis on to their children.

What do you think happens to those children when they become adults? They start their adult lives with a pre-paid, first class ticket on the victim consciousness express.

Does any of this feel familiar to you?

Why are beliefs and perceptions important?

All of the information we receive is filtered through our beliefs.

Perceptions create the boundaries we use to define the world and our place in it.

Our brain receives information and processes it through our belief filters which translate those messages into something that fits within our belief system. So if, for example, you have always heard that all rich people got their money illegally and by taking advantage of other people, every time you hear about a rich person's success, your belief system tells you that they are probably crooks and they take advantage of other people.

So, you don't want to be rich because then you would have to become a crook and be mean to other people. And while you may be poor, at least you're honest and you don't take advantage of other people. Right? It sounds good to you because that's part of your belief system. But if you actually said that to someone, they would probably ask you why you believe that. I know many rich people who are also honest and hard-working. They are not crooks. And they are kind to and generous with others. But if you believe that all rich people are crooks, then you are going to ensure that you never become rich because that would mean that you would also be a crook.

Your beliefs and perceptions also play a strong part in determining the types of jobs that you choose, the relationships you pick, your partners and your friends. Even the lifestyle that you lead today was chosen by your beliefs and perceptions.

Think about it -- if you do not have everything that you want, in all areas of your life, so that you are totally and completely happy and satisfied with your life, why not?

What has caused you to create the life that you are living today?

Were there any paralyzing events in your life that you are still crippled by today?

How do these events limit your confidence and what do they prevent you from doing or accomplishing in your life?

What areas in your current life situation are supported by your belief system?

What beliefs would you have to change in order to move forward in your life?

What are your belief systems telling <u>you</u> about being rich, successful, happy, having what you want in life, being in a relationship with a partner who loves you, realizing your goals, and having the life you want to live?

Our perceptions are like our beliefs in that they also help us define our world. They too, are developed during our childhood and are formed by the input that we receive from our parents, family, and friends. Our perceptions help us to understand our world by defining its parameters. For example, we know that grass is green. That's a perception. To someone who is color-blind, however, grass is brown. If they have been color-blind since birth, they know that grass is always brown or gray, beyond the shadow of a doubt, and you can't tell them otherwise. Period. End of discussion.

Why? Because they can't see the color green, they have never seen the color green, and they don't know what it looks like. And their perception tells them that if they look on the ground and see brown spiky stuff, there's grass there.

Perceptions give us the boundaries that define our lives. And that is a good thing, in a way. But unless we reconsider them on a regular basis, assessing what we create with them and allow ourselves to consider other options, the boundaries of our perceptions become the walls that hold us back from realizing our true potential. And if those boundaries were created around a victim consciousness, they become the fear that paralyzes you. Your perceptions exist to protect you and to keep you safe. But, they can also prevent you from moving away from the things that make you unhappy and towards something new or different, that creates joy and abundance.

My perception that going after what I wanted would lead to disaster was true because that did happen to me. But there was another perception that I developed during my years of being paralyzed and then handicapped that was hidden and had a more serious, crippling effect, and it was based on shame. I knew that dealing with my handicap was a struggle for my parents and my family. And I am sure that my mother said or thought, many times, that if I had not tried to ride that tricycle, nothing would have happened and we wouldn't be in this situation.

While my handicap was a serious inconvenience, knowing that I was the source of that inconvenience led me to believe that I was also a source of shame for them. Remember they constantly had to endure stares and finger pointing whenever I was with them. They also had to answer the question of 'What's wrong with your daughter?' when people asked, and they asked quite a lot. Whether that was from curiosity or genuine concern, I'm not sure. I do remember my parents' tensing up whenever we were in a public situation and they had to push me around in my wheelchair, or help me with my braces and crutches. I was 'ashamed' of my condition and I felt that I was a source of shame for them and for the whole family. I had a brother and a sister who also had to endure the stares and the questions about me.

Now I became doubly crippled -- going after what I wanted could have disastrous consequences and I would be a source of shame to myself and everyone around me, as well as being a burden and an inconvenience. With that kind of perception, no wonder I agonized over every new opportunity and usually either passed it by or sabotaged it before it could become a reality for me.

If your perceptions about life have been developed by an environment that is full of hidden dangers, unpleasant surprises, guilt, shame, and blame, unmet needs, and unfulfilled expectations, then your perception of life is that you had better lay low, because if not, something bad is certainly going to happen to you. And, even if you do your best to hide from life, something bad will probably happen to you anyway.

You have become a victim, paralyzed by your fears, afraid to move, unable to take control of any situation, and crippled by the memory of your experiences.

If you are a victim, you probably perceive the world as a dangerous, frightening place that will eat you and your lunch if it has even half a chance.

You may believe that every romantic relationship will end in some kind of disaster, your boss will always be critical of you, you'll never be paid what you are worth, and that you will never have enough, be enough, or do enough to ever succeed.

And, as long as you continue to believe those things, you are right and that is exactly what you will get.

You may be asking yourself why the Universe doesn't step in here and prevent all of these things from happening. That's an excellent point and there are three very good reason why this doesn't happen.

First, because we have free will and it cannot happen. The Universe is incapable of interfering in our life, no matter what is happening, until we specifically set an intention to change.

Second, because the Universe doesn't judge us or anything we do. It doesn't recognize anything as good or bad, right or wrong, it agrees with us in everything we think, do, or say. It can't override our choices, even if it's the most powerless choice we can make, the Universe just gives us what we ask for, and no more.

Third, do you remember the comment you read earlier which stated that 'everything is energy'? It's true, your life circumstances are created by your energy. If you want to change anything about your life, you must change the energy you are using to create your life.

Using that information, what kind of energy are you using to create the life you have today?

What perceptions have helped to create the life that you are living today?

What areas in your current situation are supported by your perceptions?

What perceptions would you have to change in order to move forward in your life?

Can you think of one or more ways you could change your energy, to change your life?

How are you using your energy to create
and support the life you have today?
What are your perceptions telling you about being rich,
successful, happy, having what you want in life,
being in a relationship with a partner who loves you,
realizing your goals and having the life you want to live?

Taking this one step further, your beliefs and perceptions will cause you to choose people, circumstances, events, and situations that will reinforce them.

You will unconsciously choose jobs that do not pay well, bosses who do not value and honor you, partners who do not treat you with love and respect, and circumstances where you will not succeed, because your beliefs and perceptions will limit what you attract in your life to whatever reinforces them and makes them true.

And the fears that paralyze you will stop you from experiencing the full range of joy, success, and abundance you could have because you will sabotage the process before it can fully materialize.

Think about an opportunity you didn't take advantage of at some point in your life.

What stopped you?

Where did you feel crippled or handicapped in some way, that prevented you from seeing the potential for success?

Were you afraid of the situation or unsure of yourself? Can you remember what the fear felt like?

Are you aware of how your beliefs and perceptions impact your life choices?

How are your current life circumstances evidence of your current beliefs and perceptions?

It is possible to change your life circumstances by changing the beliefs and perceptions you have about yourself and the world around you.

To do that you must start to see yourself as a VICTOR instead of a victim.

I AM A VICTOR!

Would You Rather Be a Winner or a Victor?

If I asked you for a definition of the word 'victor' you would probably say that it is a 'winner.' Yet, while these two words are used within the same context, they have a different focus.

A winner is focused on the small picture;
a victor is focused on the big picture.
The 'win' requires an external focus;
a victory requires an internal focus.

To win is defined as 'to gain a victory.' Notice the word 'a' in that definition. It means a single one. If you are focused on winning, you are trying to succeed at whatever is in front of you, like winning a contest, a job, a contract, or a promotion. It is a one-time event that you can repeat, over and over again, as each 'win' gives rise to another opportunity to 'win.'

If you are a sports fan you know that teams measure their performance by how many 'wins' they gain during the playing season. And that number changes with each game they play. The team is only as good as their current win; a single loss can dramatically change their standing and their popularity.

Winning is externally focused, requiring us to 'do' something better than someone else. Within competitive societies being a winner is paramount and who we are as a person (our being) matters less than whether we can win at something.

Have you ever won anything in your life?

How do you feel when you compare yourself to people who win?

Do you feel like a victim if you don't win at what you attempt?

I never won any contests that required physical prowess during my childhood because I wasn't as physically capable as the other children my age. I wasn't the last one picked for the team because I wasn't allowed to play sports, so I was always on the sidelines. I never had to worry about not being included because it was a given fact that I wouldn't even be considered. No, I never won the prize for running the fastest relay race, but I won a lot of contests and prizes that required excellence in other areas, such as music, math, languages, and science. Even if I was physically handicapped, there was nothing wrong with my mind.

I had to learn to appreciate the victories I achieved with these gifts, though. And while everyone admired the kids who could run faster and climb higher than anyone else, I was the one everyone came to when they needed help with their homework and the one they wanted to sit next to during a test. I could have focused on the small picture of never being a winner or being able to play the games like other children, or I could remember how much my classmates appreciated my help with their homework and see that as my personal victory. It's all in the perception and that was a big victory for me.

How important is winning to some people? Look at athletes who are willing to risk their long term physical health by taking dangerous steroids just to be able to say they were the fastest and best at a sport.

Or the people who are willing to sabotage another player or a game just to be able to stand on the podium and accept the first place prize, no matter what they had to do to get it.

Have you ever been around someone who was willing to do anything to win, even to the extent of lying, cheating, and betraying others, or forcing their 'must win' agenda? For someone people winning is everything and they will ensure that they win at all costs, whatever those costs are. We could say that they are willing to victimize themselves in order to win. That's not to say that we should not try to win but being a victor and seeking victory are much better and more sustainable options.

A victor is a way of 'being,' and it is part of who you are because while a win is an external process, victory comes from within. The word 'victor' is derived from the Latin word *vincere* which means 'to conquer.' So a victor is more than a 'winner,' a victor is a conqueror, someone who uses their power to rise above a situation. When we conquer something we overcome or rise above it by physical, mental, emotional, or moral force. Think about how we use the word victory – we describe healing as a 'victory over illness', or the achievement of a 'moral victory'. A mountain climber describes a successful ascent as a victory.

A victory describes overcoming a major challenge, life event, or a situation that represents a personal threshold. A victor isn't focused on a single win, they want to overcome, to move beyond an obstacle, they are determined to rise above defeat and make a dramatic transformation that allows them to take their life into new directions. This requires an internal change, an inward focus that creates permanent and lasting results in their outer reality.

No more individual attempts at winning a small piece of the pie -- they want the whole pie. That 'pie' could represent a set of circumstances, their personal or professional lives, or a situation where overcoming their own limitations was the only way to ensure permanent and total success.

Not only did they 'win,' they also ensured that they would be able to replicate their victorious results in the future, results that would be reflected in every area of their life and affect everything they did from that point forward. It means moving from paralyzed to powerful, and to rise from being crippled by their fears to taking confident action.

While winning involves 'doing' something, becoming a victor is a process of 'being,' a change from an outward focus on a single successful result to an inward focus on being a success in their mind and heart.
A winner enjoys short-term success; a victor has long-term successful results.

So, what would you rather have?

Total and complete victory, all of the time, in everything you do, or an occasional success? Being able to relax and enjoy your victory, or enjoying your current win while you nervously look around and hope that someone is not going to take your 'win' away from you?

An outward focus that involves working hard, every day, for every accomplishment, or an inward focus that allows you to relax, enjoy your victories and know that you can have a piece of pie whenever you want one, instead of having to grab at the piece that is in front of you because you do not know if it is going to come around again

Would you rather be a winner or a VICTOR?

And winning is temporary -- if you win this time, you may lose the next time and then you are right back where you started before you won. What's more, if you didn't win, you lost and that makes you a 'loser.' No one ever wants to be a loser and you probably don't either.

Think for a moment about a situation where there was a chance you would lose.

What did you do or were willing to do to keep that situation alive, even if you knew it was not the best thing for you, because you did not want to lose?

If you knew there was a possibility that you wouldn't win, would you be paralyzed, crippled by your defeat, unable to move, and afraid of what may happen to you?

Does the possibility of 'losing' or of being a 'loser' make you want to give up and quit before you even start?

How does this fear repeat itself in your life and in what ways does it cripple you --prevent you from taking action or from even believing that you can take action?

There is a lot at stake when the choice
is between winning and losing,
and we will do a lot to avoid being a 'loser'.

If you believe that you are a victim, then you already probably feel like a loser, so are you really going to put yourself in situations where you may lose and reinforce that belief? Probably not. You will play it safe by not even getting into the game so you do not have to risk losing anything.

Remember my fear of going after what I wanted because something bad might happen to me? I played it safe for many years by limiting my options and not going after what I wanted, just to be safe, which was my way of crippling myself so I would not become paralyzed again.

But being a victor does not work that way. When you become a victor, you overcome a situation or circumstance and the battle is personal, as is the victory. With an inward focus, winning is no longer an issue because whatever you set your mind to, focus on, or desire in life, you have already won -- you are a VICTOR.

You will succeed at everything you attempt because your standards are personal and unique, and you are not competing against anyone or anything.

Many people we consider to be victors overcame and 'made it' against many odds. Most of them didn't start out with any powerful advantages. Sometimes the opposite was true, they had no advantages at all and had every reason to fail. So they started with their dreams, a goal that they were willing to embrace, determination to continue to move forward, no matter what, and the belief that they would overcome the obstacles that prevented their dreams and goals from happening.

Whatever it took, they would conquer their circumstances, realize their objectives, and not let anything stand in their way.

When I was in the hospital, recovering from my paralysis, I heard many conversations between my doctors and my parents, where the doctors told them I would probably never walk again. The first time was when I woke up from a coma and could not move at all. In that moment, at the age of five years, I said to myself "Oh, yes I will!" And even though I could not move or walk for several years, I absolutely knew that I was going to walk again. There was not a doubt in my mind that one day I would walk and run just like other children. So I did all of the exercises the doctors told me to do, and more. I worked diligently with the physical therapists, even though some of the physical therapy was painful and difficult.

Then day I could walk without crutches and leg braces and was one of the happiest days of my life. What I learned in that struggle stayed with me because I knew that no matter what anyone told me, I could overcome anything I was determined to do. I overcame the physical paralysis but the crippling effects of that experience took a little longer to resolve.

Now I want to add something here because my dream was to be a ballerina and I probably could have done that prior to being paralyzed. But, by the time I could walk again, I was too old to start dance training, my right leg would never be strong enough to perform at ballet's demanding levels, I have less control over my right leg and foot, and I had lost part of my sense of balance, so even if I could do some ballet, I would be a very wobbly ballerina.

My choices were to spend the rest of my life feeling defeated because I would never be able to dance ballet or to find some other aspect of my gifts to use. And I did, I'm very intuitive, a gifted writer, and very smart. People admire me for those things and most people don't even know that my dream in life was once to be a ballerina because there are other things I do that I am recognized for.

In my case, my idea of what I was capable of doing and of what a victory meant to me had to be adjusted to accommodate what I was now capable of. I had certain limitations that I had to honor -- that's not a cop-out or defeat, it's my reality. I have trouble with balance poses in yoga today because my sense of balance is not fully present.

But that wouldn't matter if I had defined winning as getting around with crutches and braces, walking with support, and never being able to participate fully in life. Being a victor involved overcoming the paralysis, both physical and mental, including any disappointments and limitations, making appropriate course corrections, and re-defining how I perceived limitations so I could allow other paths and options to be just as attractive and successful to me as the ones that were no longer possible.

That's what I did. And you can overcome anything you are willing to put your determination, energy, mind, and effort towards too, when you decide to overcome your victim story, whatever it is, and become a victor. You must also be willing to make course corrections or adjustments as necessary and not be fixed on the 'big win', the one big thing that you believe is going to make you happy forever.

A victor is someone who has made a decision to conquer whatever is in their way or holding them back and to fulfill their dreams or objectives. And they realize that there is an internal process, something they have to transform within themselves, that will make this possible. They don't let setbacks defeat them and are willing to make course corrections as they become necessary so they aren't fixated on one option or solution but are willing to consider many different outcomes.

But, there's more to this. With your decision to become a VICTOR you have made a commitment to change your life on the outside by making a change on the inside, to do something different in each moment and to create the momentum that will move all of the victim energy out of your life and replace it with your new VICTOR status.

That decision alone is enough to start you on the path to becoming a victor. It means that you are taking a stand for yourself, to become a positive force in your life, to release your victimhood and live your life as a victor.

From victim to VICTOR is a choice that you have to make for yourself,
no one can make this choice for you.
Then everything in your life reflects your choice to become a VICTOR or to remain a victim.

Congratulations. Realizing this is an important part of your transformation from victim to VICTOR.

Now, how do you do it?

How Do I Become a VICTOR?

Some people are born with so much self-confidence, self-awareness, and self-esteem that they are never afraid of failure, are always successful, and they never become victims. That's great for them.

For the rest of us, though, life may be a little different. Through the process and experience of life many people become victims. Some of them never reach the point where they become aware that a higher potential is possible for them and they are never able to envision a life that is different from what they currently have.

They spend their time wishing and hoping that something better will come along to magically change their life and take them out of their misery.

How sad is that?

Becoming a victor means being able to take that first step, making the decision to do something different, and then taking inspired action to do it. To stay in victor mode you simply repeat that process, over and over, in every situation. Here's the victor process: assess the situation, set an intention for the outcome or goal, choose the right, forward focused action, and then do it.

Let me share one of my victory stories with you. A few years ago, during one of the lowest periods in my life, I was barely employed, nearly homeless, and had no money. Everything I owned was in storage, I was sleeping on a mattress on the floor of a friend's small apartment, and my future prospects were dim. Despite my excellent resume, the only job I could find was reading tarot cards in a metaphysical book store (and I don't know anything about reading tarot cards).

Every night I would go to bed and say "God, this just isn't working. I'm really miserable and you're not helping me at all. I have done my best and I can't do this any more. If you aren't going to help me, then please take me home and let's be done with this mess. Thank you."

And every morning I would wake up, look around me and say "Darn it, I'm still here." I did this every day and night for six months.

One day I decided that since my request to go home wasn't being heard, and the sadness and depression were not working for me, I was going to do something else. Instead of seeing myself as a victim in my life, I was going to be positive about my circumstances, see myself as powerful, and start affirming how wonderful my life was and how my needs were always met in an effortless way.

I decided to go to France.

A few weeks after I made the change in my beliefs (and stopped asking to go home every night), I was paying bills and decided that I wanted to go to France that summer. I wanted to go for two weeks, to a part of France I wasn't familiar with, eat great food, and stay in wonderful hotels. Now remember I didn't have any money, no credit cards, I was working part-time, and could barely pay my bills. But I really wanted to go so I just set that intention and let it go.

A few days later I received an email from someone I had known a few years before. He had been one of my marketing consulting client two years earlier and I didn't know that he still had my email address. And since our working relationship hadn't been that great, I almost deleted his email without reading it. But my little inner voice said to have a look, so I did.

And I'm glad I did because he owned a travel agency, had a tour going to Normandy (in northern France) later that summer, and needed a translator (I speak French and spent most of my childhood in France). The tour lasted two weeks, he would pay all of my travel, lodging, and meals and (the best part), he would pay me for going. "Was I available?" he asked in the email. I sure was!

The trip was everything I had asked for with a bonus, I was going to get paid for going on my fabulous vacation. So I went and had a wonderful time. What a victory! And within two weeks after I returned home from the tour, I had a new, high paying job, was able to move out of the tiny apartment into my own place, and retrieved my belongings from storage.

By releasing my victim story to become a victor, I created a tremendous shift in my energy and beliefs that spread to every part of my life.

You can do this too.

A victor decides, at some point in their life, that they are going to conquer their circumstances, overcome their paralysis, move from being crippled to being confident, to leverage their defeat to become determined, to change their beliefs and perceptions, and create a different outcome for their life.

They choose to step beyond what they have learned about life and living as a victim from their parents and others in their life, heal the trauma that has been crippling their efforts, and put themselves on a different path. At some point, whether it was when they were totally down and out, homeless, jobless, at the end of their rope with $5.00 in their pocket, or cold, hungry and tired, a victor decided that enough was enough and that they, and their circumstances, were going to change.

How did they do it?

One of the first things they did was to decide, then and there, that they were going to take responsibility for what was happening in their life in that moment, and then for doing whatever it took to change their circumstances. No matter how desperate their circumstances and how impossible their situation appeared on the outside, they were determined to overcome and transform it.

Then they began to identify which of their beliefs and perceptions would have to change so they would no longer attract what they were currently experiencing.

They had to identify what was paralyzing them and crippling their dreams so they could finally heal from it, release it, and open the door to transformation.

They had to decide that they were either going to live in their paralyzed past or create a new confident, powerful outcome for their life.

Finally, they found something to focus on, a goal, an outcome, an idea, or a vision, and used that as the central point for this process. They had already decided that anything was worth a try because whatever they were doing up to that point was definitely not working (like asking God to take them home every night).

They were not happy and being a victim had become too much work and was eating away at their energy. It was not necessary for them to know what they were going to do, how their dream would manifest, or what would happen next. All they had to do was to be willing to take the first step, and to leverage their defeat to create a path of determination.

They kept their focus on their dreams, goals, and vision and declared that whatever had been blocking them, until that point, was no longer going to be a controlling factor in their lives.

Then they took action, one step at a time, with victory as their destination.

Nothing was going to hold them back from becoming successful, happy, fulfilled and a VICTOR.

They were going to do it, no matter what it took and no matter how long it took.

Their focus on their dream gave them the ability to change their beliefs and perceptions and to create a new model, a new paradigm, for their thinking.

They became clear about their goals.

They were determined to reach their goals.

They stayed focused on their goals.

They overcame their fears, doubts, and crippling paralysis.

They did not get overwhelmed or give up when things got tough.

They took the journey one step at a time and kept moving forward.

Their mantra became:

I AM A VICTOR!

PS: And in a way, God did take me home because I was born in France and it's home for me. So my free trip to France was actually a home coming. Doesn't the Universe have a strange sense of humor!

It All Starts with I AM

I AM is a very powerful phrase. In the Bible, God uses the phrase 'I AM' when speaking to Moses (Genesis 17:1) with the well-known words "I AM that I AM." When you use the phrase 'I AM' your brain takes notice, because you are not just saying words, you are making a decree.

Every time you say the words 'I AM' you are confirming your circumstances, whatever they are, good or bad, as being true.

Think about that for a minute.

If you say 'I am broke' or 'I am sick and tired', all of the energy in the Universe agrees with you and affirms whatever you said as being true, and this becomes the truth in and of your reality. What do you think happens then? You may actually ***be*** broke or sick and tired, but every time you say those things, you reaffirm them and their presence in your life. In fact, each time you repeat those phrases you actually attract more of their energy and outcomes. And the energy responds accordingly by keeping you in those situations.

Remember the Universal Law of Attraction? Every time you say 'I AM' you activate the Universal Law of Attraction to attract whatever you are thinking or talking about to you.

One small note about all Universal laws here, they are all non-judgmental. This means that they do not make distinctions between good or bad, right or wrong, positive or negative. In the Universe, everything simply 'is'. There is no referee to act as a go-between for you, to ensure that you are only asking for the most positive, powerful, life-affirming things. Instead, the Universe sees each of us as powerful, believes we know what we are asking for, and responds accordingly.

So rather than pausing to ask us whether what we just asked for is what we really want, the Universe just gives it to us.

There is so much power in the words 'I AM' that every time you say them, the Universe accepts whatever you follow them with as the truth and then situations in your life are created to ensure that this becomes the truth for you. And, as long as you keep repeating it, it will continue to be the truth for you and for your life, and will be reflected in all areas of your life.

Over the next few days, pay attention to how many times you say 'I AM' and what you are affirming as the truth in your life.

Are you going to use it to reaffirm everything that is not working in your life, or are you going to use it to create new potentials for the things you hope for and dream about?

Are you going to reaffirm that 'I am sick,' 'I am broke,' or 'I am unhappy,' or are you going to affirm robust health, financial abundance, joy, and fulfillment?

How many times do you reaffirm the fears that paralyze you, the things that cripple your dreams and make your goals impossible to achieve?

Can you intend the fulfillment of your dreams and create powerful, victorious beliefs that support them?

How does it feel to say "I am financially secure" or "I am in perfect health" or "I am very happy with my life" now?

Even if it is not the truth at this moment, if you affirm that negative conditions exist in your life, they will continue to exist. If you create the potential for positive situations, you open the door to them.

Remember the Universal Law of Attraction is 100% responsive to your thoughts and words and acts without judging them or you.

Every time you send your brain a message through your words or your thoughts, it looks through its memory to find a corresponding message. Your brain has a long memory and those messages include everything that you have ever heard about those subjects, beginning with when you were a little child. If you suddenly begin to use different words or to say something other than what your brain is used to hearing, it pays attention.

Here is a truth about how the brain works that you may not be aware of: our brain does not think new thoughts unless we consciously and deliberately put new thoughts into our brain.

It's true, most of our thinking is habitual, the repetition of old messages and beliefs that we have heard from others or have learned over the course of our life. Most of the people we know and are close to, our friends and family, have the same thought habits that we do.

How many times do you catch yourself saying the same things you have heard your parents say to you, in the same tone of voice and with the same facial expressions or hand gestures?

What type of thought habits do you share with family members, with your friends, or your partner?

Which of your thought habits are you sharing with your children, or you notice that they have learned from you?

These thought habits are important in creating the security and stability in our lives. And some of them are very useful. Consider the thought habit that allows you to remember how to drive a car, or to tie your shoes, or to do anything that requires memory. These are things you can do from habit and don't have to think about.

So whenever the brain has a new message that it has to process, one that is different from anything that it has heard in the past, that message receives special attention. If there are no beliefs or perceptions that it can attach to that message, the brain is really going to be bothered.

And it's going to make you uncomfortable. You are upsetting its thought habit patterns and that is an uncomfortable thing because it has to create a new thought pattern to accommodate that thought.

What does it do when a thought habit pattern is upset? It gets confused, afraid, upset and angry. It starts to forget things and is off balance. And it resists the new thought pattern by trying to erase, discount, or ignore it.

Think of something that you do as a habit, perhaps it is how you get ready in the morning or the path of your commute to work. You probably do it the same way every day. For example, if you eat breakfast first and then get yourself ready for the day, try changing your routine around. Take your shower and get dressed first, then eat breakfast. If you drive down a particular road or take a certain bus to get to work, try going another way.

The first day you do this you will feel very uncomfortable and off balance. You will forget to do things, or get lost, and the process takes much longer than it normally does. Or you will feel very disoriented. We are all busy and we develop habits, which are the things we do in the same way all of the time, to help us manage our busy lives.

We create a routine (a habit) and we follow it exactly the same way so we can do it without thinking about it.

Whenever we change a habit we are creating a new thought process. It takes at least twenty-one days, that's right 21 days, to change a habit—and to create a new habit.

In fact, the first time that you say 'I AM a Victor' to yourself, watch your reaction. You're probably going to say it in the bathroom with the door shut and locked and the shower, the toilet, and the sink running, so that no one can hear you.

Saying **'I AM A VICTOR'** will probably make you very uncomfortable because the first response from your brain will be 'No, you're not. Look what happened when you tried to get that job, promotion, finish college, lose weight, get that date, pass that test …' Why? Because it's new, different, and there is nothing in your brain's memory to connect with that kind of message. According to your brain, that message cannot be true today because it has not been true in the past.

Plus, if you believe that you are a victim, your belief system and perceptions are stuck in victim mode and they are not aware of any other way to be. So, you're going to be fighting against yourself for a little while, to establish that new belief system.

Changing your thought habits can be done when you create a new thought habit.

The brain is very powerful and its mission is to keep you safe, comfortable, and secure. To do this it will adapt its actions, thoughts, and beliefs, to any circumstance that you place before it. Although it's happiest when it's processing old, well-known messages, even if those messages create chaos and unhappiness in your life, it will accept new messages into its memory if you put them there. Eventually, those new messages will be added to its thought habits and become its new thought habit patterns.

The brain also creates anything that you think or speak about in your reality.

What are you talking or thinking about now?

How would you feel if it was sitting in the middle the room right now?

Is it something that you would be proud to see or to show your friends and family, or would you be embarrassed by its presence?

The next time you start to think about something negative, ask yourself if it's something that you would like to expose to the light of day.

Ask yourself if it is something that you want in your life, for the rest of your life.

If not, replace it with something that you want your brain to remember.

Here's an example:

I AM A VICTOR!

Do you know that all of your thoughts and words have creative energy? Through your words and your thoughts, you have the power to create anything you want.

Will you choose to continue your current circumstances, or will you create something different?

How can you do this when you life is such a mess or out of control or scary?

Can people who are totally down and out change their circumstances? You bet. I shared my free trip to France story with you and it happened at one of the lowest points in my life, when I was feeling totally paralyzed, defeated, desperate, and afraid. But I really wanted to go to France, and I was tired of being paralyzed, afraid, desperate, and defeated.

Determination is a powerful force when you're in a 'sink or swim' moment. There are many inspirational stories about people who were once down on their luck, victims, living a life they hated, who transformed themselves and their lives.

How did they do it?

By making a decision to become a VICTOR and being determined to make it happen.

Consider the life of Tony Robbins, the self-help teacher, who describes himself, before his personal transformation, as an overweight, depressed, and unhappy office janitor. His childhood was not that great either so he had a lot to overcome to become successful. One day, while contemplating suicide, he decided that he was going to do something different with his life. His story is detailed in his books and it describes someone who was once a victim and who decided to become a victor. He made a decision when he was broke, alone, and feeling very bad about himself and his circumstances, that he was going to do something new--he was going to be successful.

That decision changed his life.

And he has helped millions achieve their dreams by showing them how the power of a single decision, made with conscious intention for change and combined with determination, focus, and commitment, can change any circumstances. Was he born rich? No. Powerful? No. Successful? No. But, he made a decision to change his life. He chose to leverage his defeat to become determined. And within less than a year after making that decision, he was well on his way to becoming the rich, powerful, and successful person that we know him as today.

He did it and so can you.

Right here, right now, you can make a decision that will change your life for the rest of your life. You can decide to change your life by becoming a victor. It doesn't matter if you are homeless, broke, sick, miserably unhappy, emotionally or physically paralyzed, or ready to go home (as I was). Start saying it to yourself, every day, all day, while you're taking a shower, getting ready for work, driving to work, at work, whenever you start to worry about your money, your life, your relationships, your family, and your friends:

I AM A VICTOR!

Write this phrase on several pieces of paper or index cards and tape them to your bathroom mirror, the dashboard of your car, your computer monitor, your telephone. Put one on the cover of your checkbook, in your bill drawer, on your bedside table.

Be sure to put your victor affirmation in places where you feel the most like a victim, or that remind you of your victim experiences.

Say it out loud to yourself the minute you wake up in the morning and right before you fall asleep. In order to re-train the brain to think along different lines, you have to keep reaffirming the new message so that it can create the new thoughts that will become part of your new thought habits.

You are undoing many years of victim beliefs and thinking, years of being crippled by the life events whose trauma has paralyzed you and destroyed your dreams. Remember that any new thoughts must be repeated constantly for at least 21 days, so they 'stick' with you and become your new thought habits. The brain accepts new truths with practice and repeated effort. Eventually, your new thought habits will lead to new ways of thinking, which will become new ways of being.

Try to remember when you learned how to read. Did you just pick up a book and start reading? Probably not. First you learned the names of the individual letters of the alphabet, which you then put together to read small, individual words, and then you put those words together in sentences.

In fact, you probably spent a lot of time working on the basics of the alphabet, sounds, and small words before you were able to pick up a book and read it. Were you determined to read? If you have ever been around a little child who wants to learn to read, you know how determined they can be. You were once like that determined little child, and you can be again.

This is the same process that you will use to train your brain to accept your new beliefs and perceptions about yourself and your life. So, with consistent and regular repetition you will eventually acknowledge your VICTOR status, just as you once eventually learned how to read.

While you are affirming your **VICTOR** status, there are some other words that you may use during the course of your daily conversations with others and with yourself that I would like to call your attention to.

They include the words 'could, would, should, can't, don't and not.' Also add the words 'always' and 'never' to that list. These are crippling words that you may use to describe situations that you want to keep out of your life. In reality, these words work much differently than that.

In fact, using these words actually reinforces what you do not want and they keep you paralyzed, unable to move out of your past, which is where they come from. How does it work? Read on…

Crippling Words – Could, Would, Should

How many times have you told yourself that you 'should' have done something, you 'would' have succeeded or you 'could' have accomplished your dreams?

These three words, could, would and should, are words that underline, profess, and maintain your victim status. Why? Because they imply that you have not succeeded in some area and further, that you were powerless to do anything else. They cripple you and prevent you from taking action, or moving forward in your life.

And, using them is a form of self-sabotage because it is an attempt to place the blame for the situation on someone and/or something else.

Using these words reminds you that you are not in control of your life and what happens in it, but that is your inner victim speaking.

The only way to change any aspect of your life is to affirm that you are in control of it.

How are you using these words in your life?

Notice that any time you hear the words 'could, would or should' in a sentence, there is always a 'but.' The 'but' is an important part of these sentences because it is a Blame & Shame word. We use this word when we're trying to convince ourselves that the situation is out of our control. The word 'but' is often used as an excuse for non-performance, for not meeting our goals, for not doing whatever we thought we could have done, should have done, or would have done had circumstances been different. It's how we blame and shame ourselves for our mistakes.

And it does a lot of internal damage because it keeps us paralyzed in old thought habits and prevents us from making life changes.

When you use the word 'but' in a sentence with could, would, or should, you are shifting blame and not taking control of your life.

Try to explain yourself out of a situation without using the word 'but' -- you can't. For example, you tell your partner, who is angry with you for not calling them. "I should have called 'but' I was busy with something else."

Here's another one: "I would have passed the test 'but' I didn't study."

Here's one more: "I could have made it to the interview on time 'but' traffic was bad."

How many times do you could, would, and should yourself into being depressed, ashamed of, and angry about your life situation?

And how many times do you reaffirm your victim status by using the word 'but' to remind yourself and others that you are not in control of your life?

How many of the Blame & Shame words are part of your everyday language?

How many of the Blame & Shame words are part of your everyday thought habits?

It's a vicious cycle and you can't use any of the excuse words (could, would, and should) without the 'but.'

So what do you do instead?

Start with affirming the fact that you are a VICTOR and then change your vocabulary to show that you are in control of your life:

"I apologize for not calling and will do better in the future."

No 'buts' here, no excuses, only an apology. You did it, you own it and you'll do better in the future.

Here's another example:

"My grade reflects the fact that I did not study for the test."

No excuses, no 'buts', and you own the problem and the result.

And another example:

"I overslept and left my house too late to get to the interview on time."

No excuses, no 'buts,' you are responsible and you are in control.

And you will do things differently the next time.

A **VICTOR** owns their responsibility for the situations that they create and they do not place the blame on outside circumstances. Sure, there may be circumstances that may be beyond their control (but ultimately, nothing is out of our control and everything has a purpose in our life), but to be a **VICTOR** you must be willing to assume responsibility for everything that happens in your life, good or bad.

And a VICTOR is determined, organized, timely, focused, and goal oriented, so they make sure that they are always prepared. A lack of preparation and organization is a form of self sabotage, where we prevent our success from happening by limiting our options for success.

A **VICTOR** owns the result of their actions -- they created them, they are responsible, and they provide a solution, not an excuse. In order to successfully transition from victim to **VICTOR**, you must be responsible for everything that you do and say.

So, use words that show that you are in control of your life and notice how, when you use different words, you get different results. Excuses may sound good but they don't change your victim status and they are effective on a very limited basis.

Once you begin making too many excuses you quickly lose credibility with the people in your life, and with yourself. A determined VICTOR not only owns the results of their actions, they ensure that their actions are aligned with their intended outcomes and goals at all times.

And there are more crippling Blame & Shame words that you use, every day, in the hope that you will keep everything that you do not want out of your life. They, too, have an opposite effect than what you might think … let's continue …

Crippling Words - Not, Won't, Don't & Can't

Have you ever noticed that whenever someone uses these words in a sentence, not, won't, don't, and can't, all you hear is those three words? In fact, it's even possible to answer a question with a single word: 'Can't'. And, we can use the word 'Don't' by itself as well.

Their meanings are crystal clear to everyone. The word 'Not' is even used alone to mean 'the opposite of' or in place of 'no.'

The word 'won't' is a short form of 'will not.' When used in a negative sentence, 'will not' becomes a double negative. My math teacher told me that a double negative equals a positive.

That's why sentences such as 'I will not take this any more!' have the opposite effect. Because instead of affirming that this 'will not' happen any more, I am really affirming that it is going to continue to happen. Plus, the amount of energy that goes into saying a statement like 'I will not do this again' ensures that it will happen.

How are you using these words in you life?

All of these words are very powerful because they have strong negative connotations. And, they don't leave any room for other choices or possibilities. 'I can't' does not just mean that I cannot do something, it also implies that there are no alternatives, that I will not, am not able to, am not willing to try, and do not want to, not now or in the future.

Wow. All of that in a single word.

How many times a day are you using these words in your conversations about yourself, including conversations that you have with other people and those that you have with yourself?

How often does your self-talk contain the words can't, don't, or won't?

How many times a day do you use any of these words to describe yourself, your abilities, your results, or your behavior?

Probably more than you know or are aware of. We generally speak from habit and many of the expressions that we use literally pop out of our mouths automatically, without forethought. They are also words we have learned from the victims in our family and have a strong basis in the past. The people we know, admire, respect, look up to, love, and trust may have used these words all of the time and we learned the lessons they taught us well. In fact, the more we admire, love, and respect someone, the greater and most lasting the impact they have on us, how we think, and how we act.

The downside to these words is that each time you use them, you reaffirm your victim status and you block your success, as well as any forward movement in your life. These words are so powerful that whenever you use them, your brain records whatever is behind them. Say "I can't be rich" and notice what happens to your body and your attitude. It probably sags as much as your bank account balance will if you continue to affirm that for yourself.

How many positive, fun-filled and wonderful life experiences are you missing out on because you think that you can't, don't, or won't?

Take a look around you and look at an item in the room that you are in. Perhaps a chair, a table or some other object. Do you know that your eye transmits that image to your brain upside down so that the image that your brain receives is not actually what you see? The brain then turns the image right side up and re-transmits that image back to itself so that you see it right side up.

When you use a negative word in a sentence, your brain translates that sentence so that it creates something positive. So, "I am not going to be poor" is translated into 'I am poor.' In case you were wondering, the brain does not change the meaning, just takes out the negatives to make the statement true.

As long as you affirm negative situations, you will continue to attract them into your life.

Remember the Universal Law of Attraction doesn't judge your requests, words, or actions. And, the brain is not forward thinking. It deals with the present, right now, this moment, as it tries to find a memory from the past to associate with it. If you have always been poor, in bad health, or unhappy, the brain isn't going to have to look very far to find a thought or memory to match what you just said.

It's going to make that statement true right now because the brain does not hold off thinking until tomorrow or next week. In fact, our brain is so efficient that it works all by itself -- we do not have remind it to think.

How many times have you gotten into your car while in a distracted state of mind and then arrived at your destination not remembering how you got there? That's how efficient your brain is. It drove the car for you while you were thinking about something else. How? Because it knows how to drive a car and it has done it hundreds, maybe thousands of times.

What other areas of your life are being driven by your brain's habitual thoughts, knowledge, and experiences?

How many times have you created your life through your habitual victim thoughts and then wondered why you found yourself with a mess?

The good news is that it is never too late to start to change. The brain has no opinions, one way or another, about the thoughts that go through your head. All it cares about is whether they match your belief systems, memory, thought habits, and your perceptions. And even then, all it does is match them to whatever is already there, or the closest thing to it. But the important thing to remember here is your brain doesn't think new thoughts.

It doesn't create any new ideas, opinions or beliefs, you do.

It doesn't make judgments about whether the thoughts are right or wrong, you do.

And it won't suggest changes if those thoughts are self-sabotaging, destructive, or are not aligned with the fulfillment of your dreams. That's your job.

When you change the way you talk to yourself and about yourself, you will notice changes in the way that you think and in the results that you get. You will also notice big changes in the way people speak and relate to you because they merely reflect what you think of yourself back to you.

You will even begin to notice and pay attention to how other people talk about themselves. At some point in time, you may even begin to tell people about the power behind their words.

There are a few more negative words that we will take a look at,: 'always' and 'never'. These are powerful and important words because they shape the future that you are creating for yourself.

How do the thoughts and words you use today create your future? Let's take a look…

The good news is that it is a [illegible] to change. The brain [illegible] about the thoughts that go through your head. [illegible] even then, [illegible] things [illegible] new [illegible].

[illegible] new ideas, opinions or beliefs you [illegible] make judgement [illegible] the thoughts [illegible] you do.

[illegible] changes [illegible] thoughts [illegible] with the [illegible].

[illegible] yourself [illegible] and [illegible] result [illegible] changes in the way people speak and listen [illegible] you think [illegible] notice and pay attention to how other people talk about themselves [illegible] some point [illegible] about [illegible] behind their words.

[illegible]

[illegible] about.

Crippling Words – Always & Never

How many times do you use the words 'always' and 'never' to describe yourself, your actions, or parts of your life?

Are you aware of their implications and how they can manifest in your life?

Have you ever said 'I never have enough money'?

Or 'I never get promotions at work'?

What about 'I never have a date' or 'Men/women never look at me.'?

Or 'People are never nice to me.'

If you make a habit of saying these words, have you noticed that you never have any money?

When was the last time you received a promotion?

When was the last time someone admired you or asked you out on a date?

Are people always mean to you?

Have you ever said 'I always get everything wrong'?

Or 'My clients are always late in paying their invoices'?

And have you noticed how often you make mistakes?

When was the last time your clients paid their invoices on time?

How are you using these words in your life?

Unless you are continuously affirming the positive factors in your life, such as 'I always have abundant resources to meet my needs,' the words 'always' and 'never' are part of your victim vocabulary that keep you in your victim status. In fact, the word 'never' should always be used very carefully. 'Never' means not ever, under any circumstances, not at all, at no time, under no conditions, in no way, in no manner whatsoever.

Since we live in a dynamic, constantly shifting Universe, nothing is impossible and every situation can be transformed at any time.

These are very strong words because they create your future circumstances.

And they are affirming and creating new opportunities for the very situations that you are talking or thinking about, including the ones you wish didn't exist or weren't part of your life. The brain does not register the negative tense and does its best to turn negative sentences around so that they are positive and affirming. So, if you use the word 'never' in a sentence and follow it with something that you do not want to have happen to you, guess what happens?

Here's an example, you say 'I never want to be poor again.' The brain translates that to mean 'I am poor again.' And guess what happens. Right, your financial life falls apart. While 'never' may be a strong word to you and your intention is to get rid of that particular situation, to your brain, it's a negative word that it ignores. To avoid problems, strike the word 'never' from your vocabulary. And, if you have to use it, do so very carefully so that you don't find yourself creating even more of what you do not want in your life.

Instead, focus on what you do want to happen because that is where your energy will flow and it will attract what you want to you.

Even if it is not happening right now, if you are totally broke and don't know where your next dollar is going to come from, if you are so defeated and crippled by your current circumstances that you do not know how you are ever going to rise up again, unless you use powerful words that align your energy with the outcomes you want, and empower yourself with the determination to succeed, you will not be able to create it.

'Always' means just that, all of the time, forever, from this point forward. If you have a habit of saying ' My relationships always fail,' guess what you are affirming? You're absolutely right. Every relationship you have will fail, no matter what you do. Why? Because you are creating your future with the word 'always' and affirming that every situation, from that point forward, will 'always' work out in that way. You commanded it and it is created as you instructed. Remember, energy doesn't judge, it merely responds to every you say and think.

How many times have you said
you would 'never' do something again,
only to find yourself in the same situation again?

How many times do the same things 'always' happen to you, even though they are exactly what you do not want?

For two reasons: one, because you are affirming their creation by using the words 'always' and 'never', and two, because your thoughts and words create your reality and you will unconsciously attract and create according to what you think and say. Remember that you have a brain that wants you to be right and it works hard on your behalf to create the reality that you are affirming by making everything true according to your thought habits, beliefs, and past results.

And the energy you are attracting will affirm that, both in the type and in the strength. Have you noticed how strongly you feel about the things you will 'never' do or allow to happen again, or what 'always' happens? We usually have very strong emotions around those experiences and those strong emotional energies get extra attention.

Instead of being what we avoid, they become what we attract because of a simple rule about energy -- it flows to the area of greatest force and intention. So, while you may set an intention for the positive, fulfilling things you want to create in your life and you follow it with very strong, forceful thoughts or words about what you will 'never' do again, guess what receives the most attention? If you guess the 'never' statement, you are right. You have just raised a big red flag to the universe and it overshadows everything else.

As you are setting your intentions, make sure that they get the full force and impact of your energy. It isn't necessary for you to affirm what you 'never' want to do again, or what 'always' happens, because if you keep your focus on the outcomes you create with your intention, the other situations won't happen or, if they do, they will no longer be important.

The great thing about the universe and its energy is that it doesn't judge any of those thoughts as good or bad, right or wrong. It just creates from what you give it to create with. If you're not sure what that means, look at it this way -- you can't create a chocolate cake from a macaroni and cheese mix. You have to start with the right ingredients to create the outcome you want.

The right ingredients include the right thoughts, beliefs, and words and staying focused exclusively on what you want because if you focus on what you don't want, that intention will receive energy too. And if it is something you feel very strongly about, you are issuing an invitation to the universe to help you create it.

If you are always affirming that you are struggling, unhappy, unsuccessful, and unlucky, the partnership between you and the universe has no choice but to help you create situations that mirror those affirmations.

If you believe that your relationships 'always' fail, then you will choose relationships that have no chance for success, every time. In fact, you will only be attracted to partners and relationships, in every part of your life, that will fulfill that reality. Remember the Universal Law of Reciprocity that says, "As within, so without." If you believe and affirm it, it will come to you, no matter what 'it' is.

The universe, the energy, and your mind have no opinion about your situation -- they just act according to the information that is provided, much like a computer. In fact, there is a saying among software developers--garbage in, garbage out, meaning if you write bad code, you'll get bad results.

What information have you been feeding yourself with lately, in the form of your thoughts and words? And what are you seeing in your life? Your outer reality is a mirror of your inner world.

To change what is happening on the outside
you have to change
what's happening on the inside.

What if you could change those circumstances so that you had wonderful relationships that fulfilled your desire to be loved and respected?

What if you could create a career that provided you with opportunities to grow, enjoy a generous and abundant income, and be passionate about your work?

What if you could create the life you are happy to live, where each day brought in new, unexpected and wonderful opportunities for success, prosperity and happiness?

You can.

Change your words and you will change your life.

By now you're probably saying, but I need more money, I want a great job, a wonderful relationship a long vacation, to release my victim thinking, and I am trying to make things work out.

I am so glad you mentioned it, because that is the next topic of discussion. In the next chapter you will find out why as long as you 'need,' 'want' and 'try' you will not get positive results …

Crippling Words – Need, Want, Trying

Do you need a new job, a new car, a change in your life situation?
Do you want more money, to be happier, a fulfilling relationship, or to be successful?

We all do. In fact, at any point in our lives, we all have a long list of needs and wants. Consider that if you need or want something, you are affirming that you do not have it. 'Need' and 'want' imply that there is a lack of that particular element in your life.

And you are not creating the possibility that you will get it any time soon. Remember the Universal Law of Attraction that says you attract everything that matches your energy, which includes your thoughts, words, and beliefs? It works in this instance too.

Remember how the brain/mind/universe/energy partnership works to create the circumstances in your life to fulfill all of your thoughts and words?

If you are always in a state of 'need' or 'want' your energy partnership is working overtime to create the circumstances that will keep those situations alive for you.

You are affirming a 'need' or a 'want' and the Universal Law of Attraction is bringing you situations where you have needs and wants.

Why?

Because you are affirming that you have a 'need' or a 'want' and there is no room for anything else to manifest to change the situation.

And you are not creating an opportunity for that situation to be remedied any time soon because you are not creating any room for improvement. You have a lack of something. It's true, it's the situation as it is today, will be tomorrow, and for an indeterminate amount of time in the future. And you do not know how, when, or whether you will ever get beyond the point of need or want. There is nothing else, only need, want, and lack.

Are you familiar with the expression 'Nature abhors a vacuum?' It's true. Wherever a vacuum exists, something will rush in to fill it. Try this experiment. The next time you are in your car and you pull up to a stoplight or a stop sign, observe what happens in the traffic lane with the least number of cars in it. One car will quickly pull over into it, and then another, and then another. Soon, that lane is full too. Why? Because there was a vacuum, a space that had nothing in it, and something had to rush in to fill it.

When you 'need' or 'want' the vacuum in your life is already filled with a need or a want. You aren't acknowledging that the need or want is met, you are just filling the vacuum with the affirmation that the need or want exists.

What's the solution?

Use the words "I have" or "I am" instead of saying things like "I want" or " I need". Yes, you read that correctly. Instead of saying "I want" or "I need", say "I have" or "I am" even if what you want or need seems to be so impossible that you can't imagine how it will ever happen.

There's one thing about how the Universe works that makes this possible – the Universe only works in the present moment so as far as it is concerned, by acknowledging that you are ready to have those things in your life (because you have asked for them), you are also acknowledging that you already have access to them, and you have created a vacuum that energy must rush in to fill. All you have to do is connect with them because they are already part of your field of potential.

I describe the concept of the 'field of potential' in my book, *Ascending into Miracles – the Path of Spiritual Mastery*. To summarize the concept of the field of potential for our purposes here, everything you could possibly want in your life is already available to you as pure potential.

When you believe you can have it, that you deserve it, and are determined to get it, you create the vacuum or space in your life for it, connect to it in your field of potential, and create the path to bring it into your reality.

So everything you need or want is already available to you, all you have to do is create the space in your life for it by creating your vacuum, and then you connect with it at the right time and under the right circumstances.

While you may feel silly doing this, act as if whatever you need or want is already in your life. Affirm that it is already there. This puts the Universal Law of Attraction to work for you in a positive way. And it brings forward another aspect of Universal law, and that is the concept of the present moment or 'now'.

As I teach in my book *30 Days to Everyday Miracles*, miracles (or movements in energy) happen at the time we think of them, not when they appear in our life. We set the miracle creation energy in motion as soon as we think of something, which means that it is already available, ready to manifest as part of our reality, as soon as we ask for it. There can be a delay in how long it takes for it to actually come to us but how long or short that period of time is depends on our levels of faith and trust.

If you act as if whatever you need or want is right there in front of you, the Universal Law of Attraction says that it has to happen, it has to come to you. The vacuum must be filled but not because you 'need' or 'want' it, because you have created the energy for it in a determined, positive, life and self affirming way.

Instead of saying "I need a new job" or "I want a new car" try saying, "I have a new, fulfilling, high-paying job now" or "I now own a new car that I love." Then, believe it will happen and don't worry about the 'how'. That's the job of the Universal Law of Attraction.

I did this when I created my free trip to France (remember I was also paid to go on the trip), I just affirmed that I wanted to go, was determined to go, and then I let it happen. And I went. Of course, I also read and answered the email that I received. Being willing to take action is also part of this process.

You can do this too, and then watch what happens. Once you have created a vacuum, something has to rush in to fill it.

Maybe a friend will call you with the news of a job opportunity that they just heard about.

Maybe someone will mention that they are selling a car that is exactly what you want and it's at a price you can afford.

Or, as one of my clients experienced, someone was going to be abroad for a year and didn't want to sell their car but they couldn't take it with them. They needed someone to drive the car for a year and my friend just happened to need a car. The miracle we ask for is often the answer to someone else's prayer for a miracle.

By creating the vacuum, you connect to everything you want that is already part of your field of potential and it will rush in to fill the vacuum.

And it will. And you will be a **VICTOR** by overcoming the lack you are aware of and turning it into an abundance of what will fill that vacuum in your life. But not by trying to do it because when we try, the Universe keeps us in a state of 'trying'.

Crippling Words - Are you Trying?

Are you 'trying' to make ends meet, 'trying' to do your best, 'trying' to make changes in your life?

Are you seeing any results? Probably not. Because as long as you are 'trying' to do something, you are doing a lot of work. And, your brain is hard at work creating opportunities for you to 'try.'

Remember the Universal Law of Attraction. And remember that the universe's awareness exists in the present moment. So, as long as you're trying, it will help you to continue 'trying.'

Take the word 'trying' out of your vocabulary.

I mean it. Take the word 'trying' completely out of your vocabulary and don't use it. Instead, replace the word 'trying' with words that create positive messages that allow you to arrive at a state of completion and achieve the success that you desire.

Instead of "I am trying to become financially secure" affirm that "I am now financially secure" or "I now have financial security and an endless flow of prosperity and wealth."

Instead of "I am trying to make positive changes in my life" say "I am now making positive changes in my life".

Instead of "I am trying to find a new partner", say "I have a wonderful, kind, considerate, loving partner in my life now."

As long as you say you are trying, the Universe will continue to help you try.

By stating your intention as a positive, present moment occurrence you create the vacuum, which means you create space for it in your life, and set up the energy level to attract it. Then clear away any paralysis, defeat, fear, doubt, and crippling thoughts and words so you can believe that it is happening.

Because it is.

Let the Universal Law of Attraction work in your favor. Remember that as long as you 'try' you will never succeed because you are not giving yourself the opportunity to arrive at your destination. Trying is filling the vacuum, instead of being and doing. 'Trying' is your result, instead of the outcome you really want.

As long as you tell yourself that you are 'trying' to do something, your brain/mind/universe/energy partnership will continue to create situations that allow you to 'try.'

Affirm that what you want is already in your life, create the vacuum and let the Universal Law of Attraction fill in the gaps.

Keep saying to yourself

I AM A VICTOR!

And watch the changes occur in your life. In fact, you will not only see changes in one area, they will occur in many areas of your life, like ripples on a pond.

While that may be the best of all outcomes, there are times when you just don't get what you want. Sometimes you get nothing at all and you have to make a really big decision -- you can have your own private (or public), short or long term pity party, and re-affirm that you're a victim, or you can do something else.

I'm going to talk about both in the next chapter and this is an area that I have quite a bit of experience in ….

And yet all the chances of occurring [illegible] In [illegible] [illegible] [illegible] a [illegible] end.

When [illegible] the heart of [illegible] [illegible] just [illegible] [illegible] [illegible] and realize that [illegible] victim or [illegible] can do something else.

[illegible] that I have [illegible]

When You Don't Get What you Want or Need

I would like to say that once you decide to become a VICTOR you always get what you want. That would be misleading because I know it isn't always true. There are times in your life when you won't get what you want, or think you need, and sometimes those will be things that you want and need very badly.

If you are already firmly grounded in your victim status, not getting something you have your heart set on can be very hard to take and in fact, can represent a huge setback in the life changes you are making.

Or, not getting what you want can lead to passive regret and resentment, where you think about it, replay it over and over in your head, focus on how unhappy you are with the situation, feel cheated, taken advantage of, unlucky, and unrewarded, for a very long time.

Resentment is a terrible thing because it keeps you in victim cycles by recalling the memories, beliefs, and thought habits that remind you of how awful the world is, how difficult your life is, and that no matter what you do, you will always be a victim.

You didn't get what you wanted and it may have been important and even critical -- but are you going to let it defeat you or use it to leverage your defeat and rise above it?

Approaching this kind of situation from a victim mindset often leads us to ask for what we think we can get, instead of what we want. And this conflict of interests means that we often get nothing.

I had a caller on my weekly Enlightening Life radio show who asked about getting a car she really needed and wanted, but wasn't having any success with. She diligently researched cars for sale and every time she found one in her price range and called the owner, the car had already been purchased by someone else. She was feeling desperate and depressed.

When she asked me what she should do, my answer was not to tell her that she would get the car in a few weeks but to ask her why she was looking at the cars she thought were reasonable and plain, rather than the one she really wanted.

While she was looking at low cost, practical sedans, she really wanted a higher end luxury car. She agreed and said that due to her current life circumstances -- she was financially strapped and had borrowed money from her family to survive -- she didn't want to attract attention by buying a more expensive car. So she felt she should be looking at cars that were reasonable and reasonably priced and she didn't think she could afford what she really wanted.

Feeling victimized by her life, she was trying to manifest a car through her victim mindset, instead of opening her heart and mind to the possibility of receiving exactly what she really wanted and allowing this to become an example of how she could become a VICTOR. And because she wasn't asking for what she really wanted, she wasn't getting a car at all.

Even if she had been able to buy a lower priced, more reasonable sedan, every time she drove that car she would be thinking about the car she would rather have, which was the more expensive, stylish car she really wanted.

Do you think she could have gotten the less expensive car anyway? I do. But she limited her ability to create it by thinking it was all about the money, worrying about what other people would think, and not honoring her dreams.

When we don't ask for and focus on what we really want, we limit our creative options. Remember, what you want is already part of your field of potential. So, in the case of my caller, the more expensive car was in her field of potential, the less expensive car was not. Is it a surprise, then, that she couldn't buy the car she thought she 'should' be buying?

So what does happen when you don't get what you want? Is there a reason for it? Yes and no, there are probably lots of reasons and none of them would make sense to you at the time they are happening.

Often, you realize how everything fits together long after the individual events have happened. I believe that these are a sort of dual purpose test, to see what happens when your determination is tested by something you want or need just doesn't happen, and to see what you do next. I believe our responses fall into three categories:

1. We give up and think it's hopeless, feeling even more like a victim,
2. We consider that maybe our vision wasn't big enough or was too limited so we use the test to create a bigger vision and examine how we limit our lives, or
3. We get help from someone in an empowered way by figuring out what they did to be successful, or in a disempowering way by asking them to do

it for us, which often means giving our power to them, hoping they will get the results that we don't seem to be able to.

As I shared earlier, my dream was to become a ballerina but once I became paralyzed, that dream was over. Even if I had fully recovered, which would not happen as people with Guillain Barre Syndrome retain long term nerve and muscle damage and some never walk again, the strength, balance, and flexibility required of dancers was beyond my capabilities. But I didn't settle for victimhood, I chose to nurture my other strengths and find joy and victory in other areas.

I had to choose how I was going to view my situation and either see my life from the viewpoint of what I would never be able to do and be forever a victim of those limitations, or be more proactive, not live through my limitations, and discover the things that I could do.

While the logical solution may be to be more reasonable and to settle for less, or to take whatever presents itself, if you do you're allowing your victim mindset to dominate your choices.

Focusing on what you can't do limits your options.

Finding new avenues and opportunities for your gifts and talents is a much more expansive option.

And have you ever discovered that when you settle in one area of your life, you start settling in other areas too? What blocks or limits us in one area can often become a blanket that smothers our dreams and makes us believe that we aren't capable of anything. So we settle for whatever shows up because we are afraid that if we don't, we won't have any other opportunities.

Can you relate to any of these situations:

You take the first job, relationship, or opportunity that presents itself because you are afraid that another one won't show up.

Or you are afraid to face disappointment, so you never ask for 'too much'. While you may not be disappointed in what you receive, you never feel the joy of getting exactly what you want either. And what's worse, you really feel like a victim then.

You stay in situations where you are unhappy or unfulfilled for a long time because you are afraid that you won't be able to create anything better for yourself.

Sometimes not getting what you want or need is due to timing, energy flows, and alignment, lessons in learning to believe in yourself, using your power wisely, to be confident and determined, to dream really big, and to not give up.

What you do in one area of your life you will do in all areas of your life. And wherever your thinking is dominated by a victim mindset is going to appear in other areas too.

While your powerful results will spread throughout your life like ripples on a pond, so will the negative ones.

Which would you rather have -- powerful, joy-filled experiences that expand your VICTOR status or the disappointments and limitations that accompany a victim mindset?

The choice is yours and if you really want to see positive results ripple throughout your life, then you need to step up your game and decide that you are going to be a VICTOR.

The Results – Ripples In The Pond

As you begin to change how you view yourself, seeing yourself as a VICTOR instead of a victim, you may notice some other changes in your life. For example, as a VICTOR, you may begin to see small successes appear in your life.

Your current job may improve, or you may find a new job.

Your relationships may improve, or you may create many new, fulfilling relationships.

Your health may even improve, as you are now less worried about your life and are not as stressed.

Your focus is on using your creative ability to develop a more healthy state of being.

You will find that you greet each new day with a sense of confidence and purpose and you are happier and more satisfied.

And as you become more comfortable and attuned with being a VICTOR you have more things to celebrate.

There is another result that occurs when you change your beliefs and perceptions. Others begin to notice them as well.

The previous challenges you had with your job or employer may improve.

The people with whom you previously had difficult relationships will either change their behavior towards you or they will quietly leave your life.

You may have more money, more free time, feel more positive about your life, and begin to experience life as a flow of grace and ease, instead of as a constant struggle.

As you begin to notice positive changes occurring in your life, you may notice something else -- your victim friends may begin to avoid you, they won't call very often, and you find that you aren't so comfortable around them either.

What has happened? Well, you have changed and they must now adapt to the new you that is no longer a victim, like them. You also make them aware of the limitations that they have and this will make them feel bad about themselves. That may be difficult for them at first until they learn new ways of relating to you and you will have to be patient with them. Or may make new friends, including the rich, happy, and successful people you used to envy.

This will also be true with your family. If you were raised to be a victim, then your family will expect victim behavior from you. If you do not continue to behave this way, they will not know how to act around you and you may find that their attitudes and behavior towards you will change as well. They may even tell you that you are different, that you have changed, that they can't talk to you any more.

Great. It means that you are succeeding in your journey from being a victim to being a VICTOR.

You may also find that, just as people who were not victims were uncomfortable around you when you were a victim, as you become a VICTOR you become uncomfortable around people who are victims, and who constantly talk about their problems.

The VICTIM sign that once shone brightly across your forehead will begin to disappear and you may find that the friendships that once sustained the 'old' you and that you found comfort in will no longer serve this purpose.

You may notice that you have less and less in common with your old friends and acquaintances, and even with family members.

You may even find that people whom you once admired from a distance when you were a victim, will approach you, wanting to form relationships with you.

Changing your beliefs and perceptions will change everything about your life. No matter who decides that you are no longer fun, cool, or easy to be with, continue to move forward. Acknowledge them and don't worry about what they do or say.

You have made a decision to change and you will stick to your decision, even if it means that you are going to have to deal with the discomfort of those around you who are not ready for the changes that you are making.

What you may not realize is that by seeing your changes, they become aware of what they need to change in their lives. And since they may not be ready to make those changes, they may choose to walk away from the reminder of their limitations, which is what you represent.

But you will enjoy the wonderful opportunities that become available to you, as you become a VICTOR.

When you change your beliefs and perceptions, you create a ripple effect all around you, similar to what happens when a pebble is thrown into a still lake or a pond. If you have ever done that, notice how far the ripples extend -- they will eventually go around the entire body of water.

Everyone will notice the changes that you are making, including your family, your friends, your coworkers, your romantic partner, the people at the grocery store -- everyone will notice that there is something different about you.

Wonderful. It means that the change is occurring and that the results are visible.

Keep up the good work.

You're on your way to becoming a Victor.

So, what's going on with your friends? Why don't they like you any more? Your friends are a reflection of who you are, your beliefs, your perceptions, and your attitudes. They also connect with you at an energy level that is impacted when you decide you want to make changes in your life. If you change any aspect of yourself or your life, you can expect your circle of friends to feel the effects of the changes you make.

They will either feel so uncomfortable around you that they cannot stand to be near you or they will want to know what you have done to create the changes they see in you and in your life because they want the same results.

In some cases, your friends will stop talking to you altogether or 'forget' to invite you to hang out with them. This is not a reflection on you personally, but it does reflect the changes that you are making. Instead of trying to keep these friendships alive, you need to let them go because they will not fit the new you.

Remember when you read that victims like to be with other victims? If you are no longer a victim, the people who choose to live their lives as victims will no longer feel comfortable around you, and you won't feel comfortable around them either.

A similar process occurs when one person in a group of single friends gets married. They now have a different focus for their lives than their single friends, and much less in common, so they begin to drift apart. Imagine what happens when the married couple has a baby – now their focus is on being parents, feedings, diaper changes, getting enough sleep, and spending time with and providing for their baby.

And they now share even fewer interests with their remaining single friends and the friendships end—until the single friends marry or have children, creating new points of connection. While the change in friendships is a painful result, it's part of the process of growth and change.

If you find that your friends (or family) are abandoning you because you have decided to transform your thinking and become a VICTOR, know that you will find new friends who will reflect who and what you have become now.

Remember that with your decision to become a VICTOR, you will attract people in your life who are victors. They will notice who you choose as your friends and if you keep your old friends, you may find that you have to keep these friendships separate, as your old victim friendships and your new victor friendships will have little in common.

And eventually you will quietly separate from your previous victim friends (or they will separate from you) as you move into your new ways of thinking, being, and living.

The decisions your friends make to leave you are beyond your control and have nothing to do with you. You can't control the behavior of other people, whether they are your friends or your family. The only behaviors and attitudes that you can control are your own.

When you make a decision to change, you have to also make a choice to accept any results of those changes. And that extends to the people in your life who will be affected by them.

It's OK, let them go.

You have many new and different things to look forward to as a VICTOR in your life.

Being a VICTOR in Your Life

As you adjust to becoming a VICTOR, you will find that many aspects of your life will improve. Because you now feel like a VICTOR, you act more like a VICTOR as well.

You may be standing straighter, speaking out more confidently, holding your head higher, and taking the initiative in situations where you may have once complained that no one ever gave you a chance to prove yourself.

You may even notice that you are suddenly provided with many opportunities that were once never offered or available to you.

If you are looking for a romantic partner, you may find that you are meeting potential partners who are respectful, courteous, thoughtful, and interested in you.

You may be offered a promotion at work, or a new job.

People will notice that you use different words, you take more responsibility for yourself and your actions, and you look and act happier and more confident.

These changes are a reflection of your decision to become a VICTOR. While you have made this decision in very general terms, you can also create a VICTOR attitude and energy in many parts of your life, including your finances, your relationships, your career, your home life.

The options are endless. You have now become unlimited (you always were, now you know it and get to live it).

To get started, think of one area in which you want to establish that you are a VICTOR.

Is it your finances? Then your affirmation might read "I am a VICTOR in the area of my financial security and abundance."

Are your relationships your area of focus? Then your affirmation could be "I am a VICTOR in all of my relationships."

Is it your job? Your affirmation could read "I am a VICTOR in my job and career."

Remember that this does not mean that you win and someone else loses, just that you are overcoming any and all limitations to success, joy, love, peace, and abundance, that you have been projecting onto yourself and your life in those areas.

You are also expanding your access to what is in your field of potential and opening yourself up to be able to receive more of what you want.

You change your beliefs and perceptions by creating new beliefs and perceptions and repeating them to yourself, over and over again, which creates new thought habits.

Affirmations are a powerful tool that you can use to alter your belief systems and perceptions because affirmations cause your brain to think along different lines and to process information in totally new ways.

Always remember to use the words "I AM" in your affirmations and to always state them positively and in the present time.

Avoid the use of words such as can't, not, don't, should, would, could, always, never, want, need, and trying, because those are crippling words with strong negative connotations and your brain does not get beyond the negative energy they create.

Powerful, life and self affirming thoughts move you forwards; negative, limiting and powerless thoughts move you backwards.

Your thoughts attract everything to you, affect your energy, and are powerful creation tools, so always think positive thoughts to create positive energy in your life.

In time, this will become a habit with you and you will soon lead the victorious, happy and successful life that you have always wanted and indeed, that you deserve.

Remember: YOU ARE A VICTOR.

Believe – and Be Do Act

In order for any change to be effective, you must believe that it is possible. So, you have to believe, without a shadow of a doubt, that you are a VICTOR.

At first, you may receive some messages of disbelief from your brain/mind but the time that you spend on your affirmations will help you to overcome that. All thinking is habitual and it takes at least twenty-one days to change any habit, including thought habits.

Believing that all things are possible is the key to making change happen. Look at how powerful your beliefs are -- they created the circumstances in your life that you are experiencing now.

What do you think will happen when you change your beliefs? Your life will change to reflect your new beliefs.

Here are some things to remember about the power of your beliefs:

Thoughts, beliefs, and words are the seeds that produce the reality you live in.

Plant the seeds you want to see grow and bloom in your life.

Every belief, thought, and word has creative power.

There are no powerless beliefs, thoughts, and words.

Every belief, thought, and word attracts things of similar energy to you.

You may also experience some pushback from your friends and family. They will also learn, in time, to adapt to the new you. Or not, it's their choice. And, you may even lose some friends who cannot accept the changes that you have made. That is an inevitable consequence of growth and change.

You will make new friends who reflect the 'new' you. The important point here is that you must believe that you are a VICTOR to ensure that these changes become a permanent part of your life.

Remember that it takes at least 21 days to release an old habit and to create a new habit so if success does not come to you right away (and it may not) or if you do not see immediate results from your decision to become a VICTOR (and they may not be immediately apparent) you must believe, beyond the shadow of a doubt, that you are a VICTOR.

You have made a decision and you are now acting on it.

You have decided to change your life and

how you interact with the world,

so the world has to change how it interacts with you.

Be--Do--Act is the next step in incorporating these changes into your life. In order for changes in behavior to become a permanent part of your life, it is important that you incorporate those three principles:

BE You have to become the person that you want to be and believe that the change is happening right now, even if you do not see immediate results. Believing, without any doubt, is the key to creating this principle. You have a choice to be a victor or a victim — you choose what you will be.

Be a VICTOR.

DO Do what it takes to create the space for change in your life, making all of the changes that you need to make. For example, would taking a college class or two enhance your career prospects? That's part of the 'do' process -- doing what is necessary to make the change an active part of your life. On a more subtle level, doing can include standing straighter, affirming that you are worthy and deserve the life you want to create, doing what you are guided to do so you take advantage of any opportunities that show up for you. This is also how you participate, as a co-creator, in the creative process.

Do the things a VICTOR does.

ACT Act the part. That means thinking, being, speaking, doing, and looking the part, ensuring that your appearance conveys the image that you want to portray. Act as if whatever you want to manifest in your life is already with you – because it is as part of your field of potential. All you have to do is connect to it and allow it to become part of your reality. What you want to be and to have exists in the present, not the past or the future. So create the vacuum for your victorious being and life and let the Universe rush in to help you fill it.

Act like a VICTOR and your life will reflect VICTORY back to you.

Now, it's time to do the work that will create the new you, the **VICTOR**...

Your Victim Story

Step One: Identify the Cause

Before we get into how to start living like a VICTOR, we have to take a look at what made you believe that you were a victim. This is a hard thing to do because you will have to recall situations and life events that are unpleasant, painful, or even embarrassing. Remembering your victim story reminds you of things you may call failures, of how you believe people didn't love or value you, how they mistreated or disrespected you.

And you may have tried very hard to forget about these things, even though you live with their results every day, as their victim.

Can you remember the first time you felt like a victim and what started you on the victim path? You may need to go very far back into your past to find the first situation, or it may have happened recently. One of my clients realized that her victim story began when she was two years old and her mother had gone to the hospital to have another baby.

The mother developed serious health complications and was in the hospital for a month, so my client was sent to live with relatives she barely knew for six months, until the mother was well enough to care for her. When she returned home, the mother had a new baby, who was now six months old, and who had been living with the mother while she had been gone. My client felt abandoned, betrayed, and replaced, and her victim story was born.

I have many clients whose victim stories center around the fact that they are adopted, and feel unworthy and not wanted. Others have had childhood incidents of abuse and bullying, by family or others, they have had health or physical issues that prevented them from living a 'normal' life.

My experience of being paralyzed, crippled, and handicapped is an example that I shared with you. Your example could have several different victim stories in it. For me, not only was I paralyzed but my brother and sister were not -- why was I the one it had to happen to?

One of my clients had a learning disability and was hyperactive as a child. This was in the 1960s, long before these conditions were recognized for what they really are and managed appropriately. At that time, these kinds of children were called 'slow' and 'troublemakers'. His second grade teacher was very mean to him, called him names, made fun of him, pulled his hair (and he had a crew cut), told him he was stupid and misbehaved, and set him on the victim path.

From them on, he believed he was stupid, undisciplined, and had no talent. Although he is smart, he barely finished high school. He is a very talented artist and writer but has never been able to attempt to expand those talents. His victim story, which began when he was eight years old, became his life story.

This is very personal work so take some time to consider what your victim story is as you'll be working with it in the transformation portion that is part of upcoming chapters.

To move from victim to VICTOR you have to know where the story begins, as where your victim story starts is the beginning of that path.

You can take your life in other directions once you know what you truly believe about yourself now, how you want to change it, and how to leverage the defeat of your victim status to determination and success as a VICTOR.

You will need a quiet space to work in, some uninterrupted time by yourself, and a little courage to go back into your past and figure this out. If you don't know how or where to begin, here's a helpful hint.

Start from the victim story. Use how you feel like a victim in your life and all of the reasons and ways you feel powerless, unloved, undervalued, unappreciated, unhappy, and unable to change.

Think about what someone did that hurt you to the core, that wounded your pride or hurt your feelings.

Think about where you feel you have been betrayed, used, lied to, or cheated.

Think about situations where you have felt out of control, disempowered, and powerless. Things happened and you had no choice about what was happening and no one helped you, or you felt powerless to stop or to change anything about the situation.

Also consider the victim story in your family because you may be integrating some of that into your life too.

Consider what do you wish had never happened to you and what is the result or outcome you are living with today?

Don't judge anything that comes up for you, just use it as information to help you dive deeply into the source of your victim story, and you may have more than one, so you can use that information to create the foundation that you are going to change.

Once you have finished with that, write down up to five main points about your victim story that you will use in the transformation work, which is in upcoming chapters.

Your main points should include:

What happened to you or what was done to you

How you felt about it then, use words like powerless, afraid, overwhelmed, angry

How you feel about it now

How your victim story or what was done to you then, has been repeated in your life

Where you feel limited, stuck, or blocked by your victim story.

This may take some time or you may feel overwhelmed by trying to identify your whole story, so start with the least difficult situation, or a single situation. Think of a fear or limitation you feel today and continue to ask yourself why you believe or feel that way, until you get to the beginning or to its starting point.

If this is too painful for you, you can simply write down a fear or limiting belief, or an area in your life in which you feel powerless and out of control, and move on to the next step.

Step 2: Take Responsibility

The first step in changing your status from having victim consciousness and being a victim in every area of your life, to being a VICTOR, is to take responsibility for every situation that exists in your life at this moment.

Although there may be people in your life who treated you badly, who helped create the doubt and confusion you feel, who participated in your paralysis and the crippling fear that you live with, and who helped affirm your belief in your own powerlessness, you are responsible for your reality and everything in it.

Someone else may have given you the ingredients for your victim life, but you are the one who puts them together into the victim package and then allow that package to become your life story.

The difference between a victim and a victor is acknowledging who is responsible for and in control of your reality and being willing to accept that responsibility. As soon as you step away from being responsible, you are a victim because you're in the energy of blame and shame. And you are giving control of your life and all of its outcomes to other people and situations.

When you are a victim, you say or think things like "bad things happen to me", "it's not my fault", "I don't have control over these situations," "someone made me do it." That is not to say that the things that happened to you were not terrible, that may be the truth in your life. But you are the one who creates the outcomes in your life, and you are the only one who has the power to change your life and the outcomes you have.

Making others responsible for the outcome — what happens after you were treated badly — is giving your power away. And when you are a victim, you are also an expert at giving your power to others, hoping that they will make things better for you. Then you wonder why your life is so difficult and nothing ever changes.

You take responsibility when you are ready to acknowledge that you are a powerful person, whether you know it or not, whether you use your power to create a wonderful, abundant, joyful reality or not. You are powerful. Everyone has the same amount of power available to them. It is how they use their power that determines the life they have.

The people we view as being the most powerful have one thing in common — no matter how bad things were they took responsibility for both the current situation and all future outcomes, and used their power to transform their life, focusing on envisioning new possibilities instead of complaining about how terrible their life was.

I created an amazing, all expense paid, two week vacation to France, at a time when my life was pretty challenging and I was very miserable, when I decided to take my power back. And I was doing a very good job of blaming everyone else, even God, for my life's mess at the time. And even then, I still got to go home to France, just not in the way I imagined, or had been asking for.

What do you want to do with your power?

When you are a VICTOR, you can be bold and outrageous and create a life that reflects your deepest, most heart-felt desires. As you step into your new VICTOR mentality, be willing to take responsibility for everything.

Victims give their power away and think that everything that happens in their life is someone else's fault. They play the blame and shame game and feel sorry for themselves.

VICTORS take responsibility for everything and know that by being responsible they are also being powerful and using their power to create the life they are happy in and proud of.

They also know that once they take responsibility for their reality and their lives, they move from being paralyzed to being powerful, from the limitations imposed by their crippling fear to the expansion that is possible with confidence, clarity, and courage.

You can do it -- Be a VICTOR.

Step 3: Creating the Reality

Now that you have made the decision to become a VICTOR, the next step is to create that reality for yourself. This chapter includes some exercises that will help you move from victim to victor by create a powerful path that you can follow.

As human beings we need goals to motivate us into taking action but first, we need to create a map that we can follow. Otherwise, we will want to make changes, know that we need to make changes, but we'll feel stuck because we don't know how to take the first step or in which direction we should be heading.

And we also need to know how we have been victimizing and then paralyzing ourselves, and which crippling beliefs, thoughts, and attitudes have prevented us from becoming a victor.

Here is what you will do to create your powerful path to move from victim to victor:

1. First you will describe your 'dream life', the life you wish you had right now. Here you will describe all of the ways you want your life to look so you can establish your VICTOR goal. This is worksheet 1.

2. Then you are going to give your victim a chance to speak because the small voice of denial, limitation, and self abuse that you try so hard to ignore or hide has important information that you need to know if you are going to overcome your victim thinking.

In worksheet 2 you're going to write down all of the ways you have been a victim in the past and how you want to be a victor in the present.

Each of those limiting beliefs has an opposite, more powerful aspect that you need to connect with to transform your victim beliefs.

3. With worksheet 3 you are going to write down each crippling victim belief, thought, or perception, decide whether you are ready to release it, and change it into a more powerful VICTOR belief, thought, or perception.

By the time you finish these worksheets, and the book, you will have transformed your thinking so you can proudly tell yourself that you are a VICTOR.

EXERCISE 1

For the first exercise, where you write down your dream life, you will need a spiral notebook or some loose leaf paper that you can put into a notebook. You can find helpful worksheets on the website at victimvictorbook.com. On the first page of the notebook or at the top of your worksheet, write

I AM A VICTOR!

Write it in big, bold letters.

Now, go to the second page of the notebook (do not write on the back of the first page, you're going to use that later). Your first writing exercise may take a few pages of paper. Be sure to only write on one side of the page during all of these writing exercises. Later, use the back side of the pages to confirm how your dream life aspects have materialized.

For this exercise, you are going to do a visualization of the life of your dreams that is filled with the things you want to be, do, and have, and then you will describe it in detail.

Take a deep breath and close your eyes. Imagine that you are living the life of your dreams, that you have everything your heart desires and you are happier than you have ever been before.

You are carefree, joyful, at peace, enjoying every moment of your life.

You are free of your desperation and fear, no longer crippled by the past and what you are afraid may happen.

Your life is a new beginning, waiting for you to create it.

What are you doing, where do you live, what kind of house do you live in, what kind of job, career, and relationships do you have?

How does it feel, to live the life of your dreams? Start writing in your notebook, beginning with this sentence:

In the life of my dreams I am…

And fill in all of the details. Get very specific because you are creating the scenario that you will focus on to change your life. Be bold, outrageous, and courageous. There are no limits to what you can dream or how those dreams can manifest. The only thing that limits the outcomes we create is our fear and lack of belief in our own potential and possibilities.

If you don't dream big you can't create big outcomes.

Take as much time and as much paper as you need. Remember to get very specific with the details of your VICTOR life.

How will you look when you are living the life of your dreams?

Are you happy? Are you rich, with a comfortable steady income that allows you to live well?

Who are you with, what kinds of friends do you have, describe your relationships, and how you feel.

What kinds of clothes will you wear?

What kind of car do you drive? Do you have two cars, or three, or four?

Where do you live?

What is the job or career of your dreams like?

Do you take wonderful vacations? Where do you go?

If the job of your dreams is to manage ten people in an office in Boston, or to create your own business that you run from your home, write it down.

If the house of your dreams is a two-story colonial with five bedrooms and three bathrooms, and a pool in the back yard, write it down.

What color would you paint the walls, what kind of furniture would it have?

If the relationship of your dreams is with a woman who is a gourmet cook, write it down.

If your dream partner is a man who is 6 feet tall with black hair and blue eyes and who likes to dance, write it down.

This creates the reality for you to focus on and remember that you will get exactly what you ask for, so be as specific as you can.

EXERCISE 2

This second exercise may be hard for you because it means going back into the past and remembering all of the ways you have been a victim in your life.

While you have probably done your best to forget these things and to pretend they don't exist in order to let them go and to release their impact and effects in your life, you need to make a conscious choice to stop letting them have such a powerful impact on your life.

If you don't, they silently insert their effects into your life every day, limiting your growth and success, blocking you from experiencing your dream life, holding you back in many ways, and creating many forms of unconscious self sabotage that you may not be aware of.

So take a deep breath, get worksheet 2 from the victimtovictor-book.com website, if you do not have it yet, and let's get started.

In the left column of the worksheet you are going to write down all the ways you have been a victim in the past. This may take a while if you have a lot of ways, but don't get discouraged.

Remind yourself that you are remembering these things so you can let them go.

If you are using a journal or paper, you can make two columns that look like the one in the example. You can also find these work-sheets to download at victortovictimbook.com.

You need to make two columns on the page as you will be work-ing with each individual victim experience you write. My clients have found that it is easier to get into their victim thinking and write down all of these things at the same time, and the more they write, they start to uncover things they had forgotten about. This helps them get to core victim issues, things that are so buried in their memory that they cannot consciously remember them, unless they are focused on doing this kind of exercise. If you cannot do this, and can only do a little bit at a time, do what works best for you.

Here is what your paper should look like to do this exercise, which is taken from the worksheet 2 on the victimtovictorbook.com website.

In the Past I was a victim because	**In the Present I AM a VICTOR because**

Once you have finished detailing your victim past, you can do the second part of this exercise. For each victim experience in the past, write down how you want to change it in the present. Don't worry about how you are going to do it, if it's possible, or how it is going to happen, you need to create the energy. Remember, you need to "act as if" to get energy moving.

So if you wrote in the left column that 'in the past I was a victim because I was afraid to be criticized', in the right column you can write "I believe in my own worthiness and I ignore criticism." Or write whatever pertains to you. You need to do this for each victim experience so you match a limiting, painful victim experience with a positive, fear-free victor alternative.

This exercise may take some time to finish and you may only be able to do a few things at a time. You can add to this list whenever you like, or as you can remember things from your past.

EXERCISE 3

Once you have finished this worksheet, let's move on to the final one, worksheet 3. This one will be a little easier because it's about releasing and you have already done the harder remembering work in worksheet 2.

In the third exercise, you are going to identify your limiting beliefs, attitudes, and perceptions and decide which ones you are ready to change or release.

Now before you tell yourself that you are ready to change everything right now and decide to change everything, remember that you are working with very deeply held fears and beliefs, so give yourself some time to really choose what you are ready to change now.

This is a step-by-step process and you want the change to be permanent and lasting, so take your time, and you can always re-visit the worksheet and work on other aspects at a later time.

You'll need Worksheet 3 from the victimtovictorbook.com website or your journal or some paper, and once you have what you need to do this exercise, let's get started.

Write this statement at the top of the first page:

I am now determined to change the limiting beliefs, perceptions, and circumstances that hold me back from having and living the life of my dreams.

To know what these are you have to identify them. So, start thinking about all of the beliefs, thoughts, and perceptions that you feel are holding you back.

You can include things such as

whether or not you believe that rich people are crooks or whether you believe you can be rich,

what you are afraid of,

what you think about yourself,

what you may think or know other people think or say about you,

what you believe about yourself,

where you think you are inadequate,

your fears about failing,

your fears around being successful,

what your parents and family think of you and have said to you that may have created beliefs and perceptions you think are true, whether they are good and positive, or bad and negative.

You may find that you uncover some troubling beliefs, like you don't deserve to have what you want, someone will take everything away from you, people always try to take advantage of you, people disappoint you, betray you, abandon you, or are mean to you, your friends or family will be jealous of you, or you just don't think you can have it.

Or going after what you want will have terrible consequences and your life will change forever (that was one of my fears).

If you can't think of what to write, what did your parents believe about these things because you have most likely adopted many of their beliefs as yours.

Whether or not you have been aware of these beliefs, they have been creating your life, which is probably why you don't have a very happy or fulfilling life at the moment or you know that you want something else, you just don't know how to make it happen.

Your job is to create the vacuum by imaging your highest potential and then letting the Universe help you fill it.

What you write in this journal is creating that vacuum.

So be bold, courageous, outrageous, bold, and daring, don't ask for what you 'think' is possible, reach for what you think is the most impossible, improbable and outrageous thing imaginable, keeping two thing in mind:

1. everything you ask for is already part of your field of potential so it's available and waiting for you to connect with it.
2. (and this one is really important) you will never ask for something that isn't already part of your field of potential.

That's true – it would not occur to you to ask for something that wasn't already available to you. For example, if you have never wanted a motorcycle you would not ask for one, right? That's because you aren't interested in motorcycles, and they aren't in your field of potential. And yet, if you did want one, you would be thinking about them all of the time.

So, are you thinking about motorcycles? Or horses, or a house with a pool? Or a great job? Or moving to France? Or an around the world cruise? Writing a best-selling book? Starting a business? Buying a new home? Taking a cooking course in Italy?

If you're expanding your thinking as you are reading this and you feel you need to add more things to your dream life, you can pause here and do that now. Or you can do it later.

Whatever it is, the only reason you are asking for it is because it's part of your field of potential. If you want to learn more about your field of potential, I invite you to get my book, *Ascending into Miracles – the Path of Spiritual Mastery* (available on amazon). This is such an important concept that it has its own chapter in the book and is mentioned in several others.

Now that you understand the importance of your field of potential, are you going to change what you ask for? Write down your new potentials for your life. The wonderful thing about this process is that it is very fluid, you can ask for anything you want and change your mind at any time.

Next we're going to address your limitations. These are not the things you believe other people do to limit you. These are the things you do to limit yourself. For example, do you regularly say things like "I'm stupid," or "I can't do that," or "I'm broke"? Do you feel powerless and helpless as soon as you start thinking about making changes to your life?

You can find a helpful worksheet at victimtovictorbook.com to help you with this exercise. First, divide your sheet of paper into 3 columns, like this, which is from worksheet 3:

Crippling Victim Belief, Thought, Perception	Am I Ready & Willing to Release It now? (Yes/No)	Powerful Victor Belief, Thought, Perception

In the first column on the left, you're going to write all of your crippling victim beliefs, thoughts, and perceptions. If you need help, read your dream life plan again and pay attention to all of the fears, doubts, and negative or limiting thoughts you have as you read it. Write those down in the first column.

One thing to note: Complete and absolute honesty is essential. This information is for your eyes only, so feel free to write down anything that comes to your mind. You must make yourself aware of everything that may be holding you back, so be completely honest with yourself.

Then in the middle column, you're going to decide whether you are willing to release those negative, limiting, fears, doubts, and thoughts or not. Now before you write 'yes' in every column, you need to know two things:

1. Changing your life takes time, energy, and effort and it can be overwhelming if you try to do too much at once. So think carefully about the changes you can manage now and prioritize them in the order of what you know you can do now and what will have to wait until later. You can number them if you wish, to make the process easier. If you can't do something right now you can always come back to it later.

2. A single change has a ripple effect in your life and many things about you, your connections, and what you do, will be affected by the changes you make. I suggest that you don't pick the hardest thing that you think will have the biggest, most widespread effect in your life to start with. Begin with a small, manageable change and see how you do. Even a small change like saying one nice thing about yourself every day can create a big change in your life. It's OK to choose the easy things to work on now, the harder things can wait until later and they will be easier then because you will already have started the process of change and experienced some of the results.

In the right column, you are going to work with the list of negative attitudes, beliefs, and perceptions from column 1 on the left side of the page.

Next to each victim belief, perception, and attitude in the left column, create a positive affirmation from it. For example:

Change "I am afraid to be poor" **to** "My financial needs are now met and I have abundant financial resources."

Change "I do not want to be lonely or alone" **to** "My life is now full of loving, fulfilling relationships that bring me joy, love, and companionship."

Change "I can't find the job that suits me" or "I hate my job" **to** "I now have a high-paying, satisfying and fulfilling job in which I am appreciated, valued and respected."

Change "I will never be able to have this" **to** "I always receive exactly what I want in an effortless, graceful way and my needs are always met in the most perfect, abundant and wonderful ways."

You're not pretending here, if that is what you are thinking, because there is nothing in your reality at this time that reflects the abundance and fulfillment that you described. You need to set intentions in the present moment (which is the moment where you are taking a breath) and you need to create a starting point for the process of changing your beliefs, thoughts, and perceptions.

In your reality at this minute, you may be poor, broke, unhappy, unemployed, underemployed, in a bad relationship, lonely, alone, and on the verge of financial collapse.

But, as long as you keep thinking and talking about how bad things are, you will only create more bad things for yourself.

Start changing that by creating the possibility for the good things that you want and create the vacuum for them in your life.

You can't be determined and defeated at the same time.

So choose to be determined, as it sets powerful boundaries around you and expands your creative energy, which also expands the energetic container you are building to make room for your new intentions and outcomes.

Be assured that the Universal Law of Attraction will rush in to fill them.

Now, what are you going to do with the list of the negative beliefs, attitudes, and perceptions that you used to create your positive affirmations? You can keep it as a reminder of what you are changing, add to it as you become aware of more limiting beliefs that you want to change, and proudly cross out all of the beliefs you do change when you see the results manifest in your life.

Refer to it often to remind yourself that you are willing to let go of these old attitudes, beliefs, and perceptions and create something new and better for your life.

Are you familiar with the Phoenix, a mythological bird that bursts into flames, only to rise from its ashes larger, more beautiful, and stronger than before?

You are like that Phoenix and you must get rid of the old so that you can rise up, stronger and better than before. So whatever you do with your list of old attitudes, beliefs and perceptions, don't think of it as something that you must keep as a reminder of your failures.

Read your list of positive affirmations regularly, even daily, to remind yourself of the new beliefs, attitudes and perceptions that you are creating so that you can become a VICTOR.

Write them down on a card that you carry in your wallet and read them several times a day, to train your brain to accept them as a new way of thinking.

Now, on a clean sheet of paper in your notebook (remember to write only on one side of the page) write the following heading:

I AM a VICTOR in all areas of my life now!

Write down the first limiting thought, belief, and perception that you are going to change now. Here's an example:

I am now changing my belief that I am a victim of my finances because I never have any money by believing that I deserve to have abundant and unlimited financial resources.

You can write about this daily and remember that you must believe that something is true and possible before you can create it.

Now write down a few action steps you can take every day, including your new beliefs, and read them every day.

Do you spend too much money or find that your money seems to just disappear? Then write down everything you spend, every day, so you can keep track of where your money is going and then adjust your spending according to your current budget. And as you are doing that, visualize having plenty of money to spend on everything you want to buy.

Do you want to find a new job? Start looking to see what is available and explore new markets or industries where your skills may be useful.

Good work. These writing exercises may have been difficult and they may even have taken some time. They were well worth the effort. Now that you have a list of what you are going to create and a list of what may be preventing you from receiving it, what's next?

Where will you start? Your descriptions are probably very long and quite specific, so it may be easier to pick one area to focus on at a time.

Do you remember when I mentioned the 'ripple effect' that is created when a pebble is thrown in a pond? The same effect will be created in your life once you begin to make changes. The ripple effect will extend to other areas of your life and you will begin to notice positive changes, maybe small changes at first, but changes nonetheless, in all areas of your life once you begin the process of transformation from a victim to a VICTOR. .

If the area that you want to begin to change is your career or your job, what steps can you take to begin to create the career or job of your dreams? Affirming your success and believing it will happen is the first step. You will get other ideas as to how you can make this happen as your confidence grows.

Can you take a class, work with a mentor, or expand your skills? And remember to listen to your inner guidance. Once you open the door to creating new avenues for your life and your energy, your inner guidance will help you stay on that path.

If your area of focus is to move into a new home, what steps can you create to begin that process? Can you start by visiting homes for sale that look like the home that you want to buy? Even if you can't afford the house of your dreams today, you never know what unforeseen circumstances could be put into motion to create the possibility of moving into the house you want to live in.

If you are still not convinced about how the universe rushes in to help you fill the vacuum you create by setting intentions, consider the story of one of my clients, one of the examples I share in my book *30 Days to Everyday Miracles.* They were a young couple who wanted to buy their first home in a particular neighborhood. All of the houses there were well out of their price range but I encouraged them to visit open houses, meet the local real estate agents, and let them know that they were serious home buyers. They went to a bank and prepared the loan papers so they were ready to purchase a home as soon as one became available.

Then they continued to visit homes for sale, talked to the realtors, and stayed focused on their intention to own a home in that neighborhood even though they had no idea how it was going to happen.

Several months went by with no success but they stayed positive and kept affirming that they would own a house in the neighborhood of their dreams.

And their efforts were rewarded when one of the agents told them about a house that was available immediately because the couple was divorcing and had to sell right away. The asking price was far lower than the house was worth but because they were prepared to buy right away by doing their **BE – DO – ACT** work, they were able to purchase the house and live in the neighborhood of their dreams.

Their **BE – DO – ACT** work involved visiting the neighborhood, getting to know the real estate agents, qualifying for a loan and getting their mortgage paperwork in order, and staying focused on their intention to own a home in that area. Even though buying a home there didn't seem possible at all, based on what they thought was possible, they were determined and they scored a major victory.

Remember, you have to **BE -- DO -- ACT** to make any kind of transformation happen. So, take a leap of faith and get started. You can start by writing down some steps that will help you move towards your goal, give yourself some action items that you can do, starting today, to get the energy moving in your life.

Who or what do you have to BE -- and this includes your beliefs.

What do you have to DO -- this is the simple, everyday work, that prepares you for the outcome.

How do you have to ACT -- this includes taking action, such as looking at homes, or talking to people, it also means using positive affirmations, paying attention to your beliefs and your self talk, and acting 'as if' your miraculous victory has already happened.

When you set your intention and use powerful words such as “I have” and "I am” you create a vacuum that the Universe rushes in to fill. Anything and everything is always possible.

Now you have a list of affirmations that will create the prosperity, happiness, and success that you deserve, you are proclaiming that you are a VICTOR at every opportunity and you are watching your dreams materialize in front of you.

Is there anything else?

Just a few more VERY important things. Once you know these, you will have the keys to creating a powerful, fulfilling, determination led, victorious life.

Have an Attitude of Gratitude

You may not feel that you have much to be grateful for at different points in your life and your current situation may appear to be challenging and even impossible. By being grateful for everything in your life you affirm your power.

When you are grateful for what you have, even if it is something you have to struggle to be grateful for, you acknowledge that you used your power to create it. Remember that you use your power to create every aspect of the life you have at this moment.

The power you used to create the life you have now is the same power you will use to create a new and different path for your life.

And as soon as you acknowledge your power, you connect to it and can then create a new and different reality.

What do you have to be grateful for? You are alive, breathing, you have eyes that allow you to see the beauty in the world, and you may have a loving partner, family, and friends.

How can you be grateful for your unhappiness or the situation you are in right now? Every situation has a lesson for us, which we must master and understand in order to release it and move forward. We did something to get ourselves into the situation, and gratitude is one of the things that will help us get out of it.

Without gratitude, we are not acknowledging our responsibility for the creation of our reality. And then we are firmly in our victim mentality and affirming that we don't have control over our own life or how it is created. If we didn't create our reality, then who did?

When you blame others for your problems and unhappiness, you are saying that they are more powerful than you are, and that they have the power to create your life. You are the only one who has the power to create your life unless, of course, you give your power away to others, and expect them to create joy, love, and abundance for you.

Gratitude is the first step towards releasing victim beliefs to become a VICTOR.

When we make gratitude a daily practice we stay connected to our power and by being grateful for what we have we stay open to receiving the blessings that come to us when we use our power in powerful ways to become a VICTOR. You may not like the life you have at this moment but you created it with your own power and you can use your power to transform it.

Each time you notice something in your life that you are unhappy with, you acknowledge that your energy has shifted and you are ready to make a change.

This is an opportunity to become a VICTOR.

Otherwise, you remain a victim.

And the changes you make in your life will inspire those around you to do the same. Be sure to recognize and celebrate the small successes and blessings that you receive and remember to say thank you.

A school friend wrote the following poem in my yearbook many years ago:

From the day you were born until you ride in a hearse,
Things are never so bad that they couldn't be worse.

I don't know who wrote those lines, but every time my life seems to be taking a turn for the worse, I look around me and recognize my blessings. Then I say 'thank you,' for the many things that I have to be grateful for which for me includes the ability to move and to walk, something most people take for granted.

Extend your gratitude to the things you may take for granted because the little things you do every day may be impossible for others. Another friend shared an African proverb with me that reminds me to extend my gratitude to everything in my life, as nothing is insignificant. Here's the proverb

"I cried because I had no shoes and then I met a man who had no feet."

That's a powerful gratitude reminder, isn't it. Extend your gratitude to everything and you will be rewarded with more things to be grateful for.

Gratitude is returned to you tenfold,
so be grateful for everything you have,
in each moment, and you will receive
even more to be grateful for.

I AM A VICTOR!

Forgiveness – The Victim or Victor Way

If you truly want to move out of being in victim consciousness and become a VICTOR and to lead your life in a self-directed way, with the determination to succeed, you must be willing to forgive.

Before discussing how to forgive and what that entails, it is important to understand the concept of forgiveness, looking at what it does and doesn't mean. Many people balk at offering forgiveness because they believe that forgiving someone is an acknowledgement that what the other person did was acceptable. That is not the case. Forgiveness is not a judgment of what someone else did and is certainly not an acknowledgement of its acceptability.

Forgiveness is possible when we are determined to no longer carry the burden of anger, pain, fear, shame, guilt, and suffering through the remainder of our current lifetime and into the next.

The choice to forgive or not determines whether we will live powerfully in the present moment or powerlessly in the past.

Everything that we believe is unforgivable is a reflection of something that has happened in the past. And each time we remember it in anger, fear, or regret, we are taking a step backwards into the past.

Victims live in the past. VICTORS live in the present moment.

To be powerful and in the present moment, you must be willing to forgive and let go of the energy that keeps you defeated, powerless, and tied to the past.

And here's another piece of information that may change how you look at forgiveness. We think that forgiveness is an emotional process and that is partly true because we have a lot of emotional energy invested in the situation that we find hard to forgive, much of it stuck in the details of what happened in the past. Once we resolve our emotions about a situation, person, or event that has caused us pain and grief, we feel better, even though we may have a hard time dealing with the 'other person'.

Forgiveness is actually energetic and it is the energy of the situation that we are releasing when we forgive. Of course there are emotional implications and we cannot deny the emotions and feelings we have around that experience. But we don't have to excuse or overlook someone's bad behavior, or invite the person or people involved back into our lives. You can forgive someone you never want to see or speak to again. But not forgiving limits our movement and restricts our energy flows, not those of the other person.

There is another, more subtle aspect to forgiveness and that is how we approach it, as a victim or a victor, and whether we seek it or grant it. Seeking forgiveness is the victim way, in which we ask for forgiveness from someone by seeking redemption - we want the other person to regret their actions, to feel genuine remorse, to show us they didn't mean it, and to ask for our forgiveness for what they did.

We do this by opening forgiveness opportunities, usually by victimizing ourselves again and hoping that they won't repeat their past behavior. Of course they usually do and we then feel even more disempowered, abused, victimized, and taken advantage of.

Forgiveness is an act of power; redemption is a reminder of our powerlessness. We won't get the same result when we seek redemption because the real disconnection and emotional and energetic clearing that we get from forgiveness is not there and cannot be given to us by someone else.

The VICTOR way of forgiveness is to grant forgiveness, to give it to others as a sign that we no longer want to participate in the energy of this situation with them, and to ourselves as a way of clearing our own energy and ridding ourselves of the ghosts of the past.

We don't need to let someone have a second chance at repeating their prior behavior because it doesn't matter. We begin in the present moment where we want to be free and clear of the past, and go forward from there.

As you are completing this chapter, ask yourself whether you want redemption, which is proof that someone can behave differently and that they are sorry for their actions, or true forgiveness, where you accept them as they are and decide what you want to do to rid yourself of your own baggage.

You won't find forgiveness through the redemption path, but you will find redemption for yourself, when you realize that you don't need to give someone a second chance at being your teacher in your lessons of self worth and self empowerment.

Everything we don't, can't, or don't want to forgive is a source of paralyzing anger, resentment, and fear that cripples our dreams.

Every time we remember something as being unforgivable, we are re-empowering what was once a source of pain, defeat, and powerlessness.

The opposite of forgiveness is resentment, which is from the French word 'ressentir' and means to feel again.

Rather than asking yourself if you should, can, want to, or will forgive, ask yourself if you want to re-empower all of your sad, angry, and frustrated emotions around that person or situation.

How long do you want to live in that emotional soup?

How long do you want to carry that emotional baggage and continue to live with its results?

If it is a situation that has victimized you, how much longer do you want to feel and live like a victim?

And, if you knew that a single act of forgiveness, which is releasing the emotional energy, stood between you and the manifestation of your dreams and the life you want to live, would it make the process easier for you?

What you cannot forgive is what is standing between you and the fulfillment of your dreams. Does that change your mind or opinion about forgiveness?

Once we take the emotions out of forgiveness, we can view it in a new way and see it as a way that we release energy that we are no longer willing to carry because we don't want it to continue to create our life under its terms.

Forgiveness begins with our willingness to forgive. Once we are willing, we can do a formal forgiveness process that shows us and the Universe that we are willing to carry through with this effort. One of the best ways to do that is by writing a letter of forgiveness. The instructions for that are provided later in this chapter. While this is not the only way of doing that, I have found that writing this down, actually putting it on paper and creating a ceremony for release validates the process and creates closure and completion.

This process can take a little or a lot of time, depending on the number of people you want to forgive and how much you feel you can forgive them, and yourself, for. You may be able to complete this in one sitting or it may take several efforts.

Remember, you create your reality and are responsible for everything in it. This may be a stretch to wrap your head around, but you have to take responsibility for everything in your reality. Even, and especially, those things that you couldn't possibly imagine you deliberately created or attracted because they were so awful.

What did you need to learn from them?

What did you feel you needed to atone for?

Before you judge your choices based on a single lifetime of events, you have to look at your life as a continuum of energy, that exists far beyond your conscious awareness in this moment. It's the many themes of being the victim and the aggressor, the abused and the abuser, that create the reasons for our choice of situations and experiences in each lifetime.

You may do it once or several times, depending on how much you are able to forgive at a time. It does not matter how many times you do it or how long it takes, when you feel comfortable with the process and with your progress, you will know that you have finished the forgiveness process.

How do you know? Once you have completely forgiven someone you can look at or think about them with compassion, be aware of their fears, and think of them without anger. Compassion allows you to accept that everyone does what they are capable of at any time, no more and no less.

If someone could have been nicer to you, they would have been nicer at that time.

If they could have been more respectful, they would have been more respectful at that time.

If they could have loved you more, been kinder, more compassionate, been more aware, they would have done those things at that time.

Everyone does what they can, to the best of their ability, all of the time, even if you think their best is not very good at all.

And with forgiveness you can feel unconditional love which has no emotional energy attached to it. Unconditional love is an energy, not an emotion, and it has a neutral emotional level which means that there is no emotional energy associated with it. It is completely non-judgmental, which means that it has no opinions about anything.

Good or bad, right or wrong -- those are judgments. It's hard for us to understand the concept of non-judgment because we're conditioned to judge everything and some judgments are good and useful. But when we judge anyone or their actions, no matter what the circumstances are around them, we are out of the energy of unconditional love.

You do not have to like someone you love unconditionally, you just have to accept them as they are. Whatever they have done to you is part of the karma you share and once you release it, your part in it is over.

You do not have to see them again, talk to them, or acknowledge their presence on the earth. With true unconditional love, you can be in the energy of compassion and have no emotional connection or attachment to them or to anything that has happened with them.

To begin the process of forgiveness, take a piece of paper and write down the name of the person you want to forgive and then detail everything you want to forgive them for, which includes everything they have done to you and all of the experiences you have had with them.

As you begin to open up to this you may find yourself remembering things from the past that you did not even know you were angry or upset about. Just write until you feel you have written everything down. Write down another name when you have finished with the first one, and continue writing until you run out of names or you run out of memory.

You can include anything, such as an old boyfriend who dumped you, your parents for not loving you enough, a former friend who embarrassed you — anything and everything that comes to mind.

Be sure to include the things that you believe are 'unforgivable' and after years of working with clients, I can tell you that some people have experienced some very awful things in their lives. But, at some point, we need to let go of even the most terrible of our traumas so we can be clear of their energy and live our lives on our own energetic terms. Otherwise, we are always living within the energy of our fear, shame, and trauma.

No matter what it is, nothing is unforgivable if you look at it in terms of the energetic burden that it imposes on you. If you are struggling with something you think is unforgivable, ask yourself how long you are willing to carry the burden of that energy and all of the effects and impact that it has on your life.

And forgive yourself as well; write down what you want to forgive yourself for. We have all, from time to time, said or done hurtful things to others, including ourselves.

Perhaps we were unkind to someone in school, or treated a friend badly -- there are many things that we do unintentionally to hurt others.

Or we judge ourselves harshly for something we did or didn't do.

Maybe we speak to ourselves in an unkind, harsh way.

Or someone received something we believe should have been ours and we are angry and feel that we could have done better or tried harder.

Maybe you think you made bad decisions in relationships, you chose unreliable, unkind, and unworthy partners, and you are angry with yourself for making those choices.

Or someone made a choice that impacted our life in a hurtful way and we resent them for their choices and ourselves for trusting them Later, we can spend a lot of time beating ourselves up emotionally about those types of incidents.

Have you ever had thoughts like "I should not have done that," or "I should never have said those things," or "I wish I could have done that differently"?

Have you had those thoughts about someone else, that they should not have done or said thing, or you wish they would have done things differently? Those thoughts create the defeat, doubt, and fear that keep us in the past and in our victim status and energy. They also paralyze us with anger, resentment, and sadness.

We need to forgive ourselves, as we have forgiven others, and release ourselves from our own negative beliefs and thoughts. Each of us is responsible for our reality, so we should also forgive ourselves for creating the situations that caused us pain.

When we remember that we create every aspect of our lives, we release others from blame, and focus on our healing and on moving forward.

Healing cannot happen until we are willing to acknowledge our own power and stop blaming others for all of the things that happened to us, no matter what they were.

Once we can forgive and be aware that there are other ways of being, such as acceptance, compassion, and unconditional love, we can relate to others in different ways. This also invites more loving, fulfilling, kind, compassionate, gentle, supportive, and caring people into our life too.

Then when you feel you have written enough names and everything you feel has been done to you, write down what you want to forgive each person for.

You can write this down in sentence format, for example:

Michael, I forgive you for leaving me and myself for creating this situation.

Mom, I forgive you for being critical of me and myself for creating this situation where I have accepted your truth as my own.

Leslie, I forgive you for embarrassing me in front of my friends and myself for creating this situation.

I forgive myself for not having more faith in my abilities.

If you fill the page, start another piece of paper. Transformation and becoming a VICTOR is a giant step in healing, so let's take a giant step and get as much healing completed as possible. Take your time and if this gets too hard, stop and take a break and come back to it again later. If you arrive at a stopping point, complete the exercise and do it again at a later date.

Once you have completed this exercise, read through your list out loud, reading the person's name and what you are forgiving them for and then state that you are now ready to give them unconditional love. For example,

"Mom, I forgive you for always criticizing me and I am now ready to release you and myself with unconditional love."

"Michael, I forgive you for leaving me and I am now ready to release you and myself with unconditional love."

Then, you are going to tear up or burn your list (safely please) to complete the forgiveness and release yourself and them from the situation. If you decide to burn your list, get a large, fireproof container and go outside, if possible. You will also need some matches, a large jar or glass of water and some salt or sand, to put the fire out if necessary. Please be safe while doing this, do not burn your list indoors, near flammable materials, or in an area where you can set plants or building materials on fire.

When you have prepared your burning area, take your list and tear it into small pieces as you say:

"I now release all of you and myself from any and all karmic relationships, cycles and connections, across all lifetimes and in all directions of time. I now forgive and release myself for anything I have done to you, in all directions of time and across all lifetimes, which created the belief that I deserved this.

I now forgive and release you for anything you have done to me, in all directions of time and across all lifetimes, which created the belief that you deserved this or should act in this way towards me.
I now forgive you and love you unconditionally and release you to live your lives in peace.
I am now a VICTOR and live powerfully in the present moment where I create a life of unlimited abundance, joy, peace, and love."

Then put the pieces of your list in the fireproof container and light them with a match. As they burn, imagine that the smoke carries away all of the pain and emotion of the experience, as well as the painful memories. When the paper is completely burned and cool, take the ashes and bury them in your garden or sprinkle them in your yard. You can also take them to a place that you consider to be sacred and scatter or bury them there.
NOTE: You do not have to burn your list, you can keep it if you wish, but burning does help release the energy and there is something very satisfying in watching the list go up in flames.

You are free. If you find that you think of these incidents occasionally, remind yourself that you have released them and they are gone. It will take some time before you train your mind to release all thoughts of the past, but time and practice will make that happen.

You may have to do the exercise more than once if you feel that you are not complete with the forgiveness and sometimes beginning this process allows you to uncover multiple layers and levels of painful memories. You will know that you are complete when you are able to think about these past incidents with compassion, or when you do not think about them at all.

You are a VICTOR, a powerful person in control of every aspect of your reality. Live your life in the present moment, be powerful in your transformation, true to your intentions, remember to

BE the powerful person you are,

DO what it takes to keep the energy flowing in your life, and

ACT as if everything you ask for is already yours, because it is.

Now focus on creating the life of your dreams. Dream big, create the big vacuum so the Universe can rush in to fill it with you.

And you will create the joy, abundance and love that you have always wanted and live a miraculous, joyful, victim-free life. Do you want to be loved and valued by others? Sometimes we call that wanting respect, but it is really a measure of what we want others to think, believe, and say about us.

The word 'respect' means worthy of a second or a deeper look, or being in high regard. You can create the respect you want by first respecting yourself and creating your own foundation of self worth and value in your life.

R – E – S – P – E – C - T

We all want respect from the people whom we think should respect us. But what we really want when we say we want respect is to be valued, honored, cherished, treated with kindness and consideration, and to receive the acknowledgement of our worthiness, and acceptance of who we are.

We don't say this out loud to the people we want it from but we wish for it silently and sometimes desperately, wondering why people don't act like they love, honor, and respect us. Then we become a victim and lose sight of our dreams because we are too busy trying to get love, honor, and respect from others so we know that we are worthy, deserving, valued, and valuable.

And we also want it from people who probably can't or won't give it to us. Remember that everyone does as much as they can in every moment. They aren't hiding any of their energy from us; what we receive from them is all they have to give us.

We can get the love, honor, and respect we want but we have to know how and that involves two simple steps:

First, other people are a mirror of our own energy and they give to us based on what they see within us. Simply put, everyone reflects our own energy back to us. So if we don't love, honor, and respect ourselves, we aren't going to be able to convince anyone that we deserve those things from them. And we won't connect with people who have the ability to give us the love, honor, and respect we want.

Second, we have to create the energetic boundaries for what we want from others. If you have listened to my radio show or classes, I talk about energetic boundaries often and why they are so important. They exist to keep our energy in and not to keep others out.

By setting energetic boundaries you create parameters for how others' energy enters and flows in your space and you maintain control over where your energy is flowing.

And here's a powerful way to do that, using my favorite affirmation that is used by millions of people around the world:

Everyone in my life loves, honors, and respects me and everything in my life is a source of love, peace, and joy.

Once you say that often and believe it, you create an energetic boundary around you that lets everyone who comes near you know that they must be able to love, honor, and respect you. Those who can do that will easily enter your energy space. Those who cannot have the choice to either rise to the occasion or to turn around and walk away. It's their choice and there is nothing you can do about it but by having the boundary you give them the choice. And you keep your own energy intact.

Try it, it works very well, as thousands of people have told me. .

You can use this affirmation to change the energy in your life, to help others know how to manage their energy around you and you will manage your own energy with it.

Everyone in my life loves, honors, and respects me and everything in my life is a source of love, peace, and joy.

Be a VICTOR in your life by acknowledging your own value and worthiness. Then you will attract people who can see that in you and treat you with the respect you want and deserve to have.

But for all of this to happen, you must make a big choice, to get out of the valley of defeat and start the climb towards the peak, which represents your success. To reach the peak, you must first be willing to leave the valley.

Moving from the Valley to the Peak

If you have ever been in the 'valley of despair', where nothing seems to work, nothing goes right, you can't make anything happen, and every day brings new challenges, you know that it is a terrible place to be.

I know, I have been there before and there were times when I felt like giving up and admitting defeat. I wasn't sure what 'giving up' actually meant when I was in the valley of despair, but when every day is a challenge, we eventually run out of steam and don't know what else to do.

Those are the times when we have to choose to either press on and try new solutions or keep doing the same things and hoping for different or better results. I now know that at some of the lowest points in my life, when I stayed in my victim mindset, I didn't create powerful results.

It was my decision to shift into VICTOR mode that created movement and transformation. And that took a big leap of faith because nothing in my life led me to believe that things could get better, I just had to get so tired of being in dire straits all of the time that I was willing to try something different.

Change can be scary and when we try to make changes that are very new and different, something has to happen to make where we are uncomfortable enough to want to try something new. Here's a truth that I have shared with many clients,

We make changes when

the pain of staying where we are

becomes greater than our fear of change.

While we may want change badly, we have to get over our fear of change first, before we allow change to happen.

We're all afraid of leaving the relative comfort of our comfort zone, which is not always where we are comfortable, it's where we are surrounded by what is familiar, known, safe, and predictable.

As soon as we step out of that comfort zone we are in the new and unfamiliar territory of our discomfort zone and unless we know that we definitely do not want to return to what we just left, we will see that as an option, until it is no longer an option.

How painful does your life have to become before you are willing to let go of your victim status and consider being a VICTOR?

The answer lies in how much pain you can tolerate, how willing you are to change, and how valuable a new beginning is to you. It also depends on how much you are empowered by your victim story and how willing you are to find new sources of empowerment.

Why would we consider being in pain when we can be free from it? Our willingness to be pain-free depends on how empowered we are by our victim story and how we use it to justify our powerlessness. If being a victim is all we know and have ever known, from the examples we had in childhood through our life experiences as adults, then pain is what we expect as a result in every situation.

And if being a victim is how we get attention from others and that's valuable to us, then it will be hard to change it unless we replace it with equally empowering ways of being.

Until we decide that we won't live in pain any longer, we will expect and accept pain as part of our life.

But deciding to be pain-free is new, unfamiliar territory and without an example to follow, of someone we know and trust doing it successfully, we have to choose between our pain-filled comfort zone or a new and different lifestyle and way of being that we may not have the confidence or experience to begin.

Pain is very empowering if it is used to create sympathy and to justify a victim status.

Do you know someone whose uses their drama stories to get others involved in solving their problems?

Have you ever known someone whose life was a series of bad choices and bad luck, and they go from one person to the next, getting attention and pity when they share their story of how unlucky they are and how terrible their life is?

While you may not think that is a very powerful way to live, it's how they get their power and energy needs fulfilled. If that person is you, how do you feel when someone sympathizes with you, offers to help, and gives you their support and attention?

How would you get attention if people were not feeling sorry for you or trying to help you solve your life's problems?

Pain is a thought habit that can be changed but first, the pain of victimhood has to be a less empowering alternative than being a pain-free victor. We have to believe that we can feel just as empowered and powerful as a victor, that we can have the attention and value we need and want from others by being pain-free.

Here's a quote I often share with clients who are struggling to release their pain and to rise above its paralysis:

To reach the peak
you must be willing to
get out of the valley.

The valley is where you feel weak and powerless, paralyzed by your fear, and where you are a victim. The peak is where you are a victor, powerful, and confident. The movement from the valley to the peak begins in your mind, once you decide you can be more empowered as a victor than you are as a victim.

Yes, it means that you stop sharing your victim story, you embrace your power, you shift the energy you are using to empower your life, and that you forgive and practice gratitude. But the rewards are great, when you see them as being more valuable than what you have been rewarding yourself with until this moment.

Are you willing to consider moving towards the peak now?

Then make a choice to get out of the valley by deciding that you are going to become a victor.

Being a victor is empowering when being a victim becomes less empowering.

And once you decide to become a victor, the past no longer matters. Don't worry about what happened yesterday, the week or month before, or decades ago. Live in this moment, as it is the only one you have any power in.

We can live in the past or in the present, but we can't live in both worlds at the same time.

Choose to be empowered in the new and uncharted territory of the present rather than the familiar, unsatisfying past that didn't make you happy then and doesn't make you happy now.

How can you start believing that your needs can be met with great abundance, that your options are unlimited, that you can have all that you want and stop worrying about whether your prosperity well will run dry?

By shifting your beliefs about there being ‘enough’ to knowing that there is plenty. Those words do not have the same meaning and the difference is profound when you are moving from victim consciousness to victory mastery.

Moving From Enough to Plenty

Victims share a common belief, that there is never enough for them. Other people get what they want, win the lottery, enjoy the great jobs, earn a big salary, find their perfect partner, are happy and fulfilled, and they get all of the 'good stuff' so there is none left for anyone else.

I remember thinking, many years ago, that when the life manual was handed out I didn't get a copy because I never seemed to 'get' life like other people. They just knew how to work with the system and get what they wanted and there was never enough for me.

Now I realize that was how I perceived things because I looked at life from my victim viewpoint which always affirmed that my life was hard, limited, challenging, and I had to choose from life's crumbs because other people got to the table first and helped themselves to as much as they wanted.

Or, I got what others didn't want or could only choose from the challenging and limited options because all of the luck and joy went to someone else.

And if you have struggled and suffered in your life you probably have plenty of examples of how there is not enough for you, how your life is harder or more challenging than that of others, or how you just seem to always be in the wrong place at the wrong time. If you have ever stood in line at the movie theatre (before there were online ticket sales) and you finally get to the ticket window only to be told that the person in front of you purchased the last ticket, you know what I mean.

One of the ways to shift from your victim story of there not being enough for you or you never getting enough in life is to stop using the word 'enough'. Instead, use the word 'plenty'.

When you focus on there being enough, you are limiting your options to a very small window of limited opportunities. With a focus on 'plenty', the opportunities are unlimited. Think about the movie ticket example. If there are enough tickets for you to get one, then you may get the last ticket. If there are plenty of tickets, then you can buy one or more and so can everyone else.

Having enough limits you to an amount that just meets your needs, with nothing left over.

Having 'plenty' expands availability into abundance and having an ample supply so your needs are met and there is a lot left over.

Think of the difference between these statements:

I have enough money to pay the bills this month.

I have plenty of money to pay the bills this month.

I have enough energy to get through my day.

I have plenty of energy to get through my day.

Which of those statements sounds like there is not only enough, there is so much available that there is extra left over?

Which of those statements applies to you and to your life?

Are you always struggling with 'enough' or do you have plenty?

Are you always trying to make ends meet or do you have plenty of time, energy, money, and everything else you need so that you do not worry about running out of time, energy, money, or anything else?

If you define your life's opportunities with 'enough' you will never have more than enough to get to that place where you can relax, enjoy yourself, and consider blessing yourself with something extra, like a wonderful vacation, a fabulous job, a great relationship, or doing something special for yourself or the special people in your life.

As a victim, how often do you say or think that there is not 'enough' for you?

In how many ways do you feel that your efforts will always fall short of what you need?

When you always say you have 'enough' you limit yourself to exactly that. For example, if your monthly mortgage or rent is $1000 and you set your intention for 'enough' to meet your payment, you will get exactly $1000 or maybe a tiny bit more. But if you set your intention to have plenty then you could get many times that amount, with much less effort.

How do you feel when you say the following statements:

I intend to have enough.

I intend to have plenty.

We live in an unlimited Universe where everything exists in abundance and this means that there is plenty of everything available to us. But in order to access that unlimited abundance we need to move from the idea of 'enough' to the idea of 'plenty', and allow ourselves to receive it.

If you have read my work on the Universal laws, you know that the opposite of abundance is not lack. In an infinitely abundant Universe lack cannot exist as there is always an abundance of everything.

The opposite of abundance is limitation, which means that although there is plenty of everything that is always available to us we limit our access to it through our victim thinking.

When we shift from victim to victor we move from limitation to abundance and from having enough to having plenty. Review the chapters that discuss the Crippling Words, as those represent your victim thinking. And when you know that there is always plenty of everything for you, your victor status and your victorious life become possible.

There are just a few more topics to discuss so you can be fully present as a victor in your life and the next topic discusses how to be in the present moment and what that means.

The Power of the Present Moment

One final note about the process of moving from victim to victor in your life -- you are at your most powerful when you live in the present moment.

Yes, bad things may have happened to you in the past, your childhood may have been terrible, your marriage or relationships may have been unfulfilling, your friends and family may have treated you disrespectfully, you may have memories of some very hurtful incidents or situations, but that happened in the past.

As long as you remember them, feel bad about them, and wish that they had been different, you are stuck in the past. And you will repeat them in the present until you stop thinking about the past and trying to reinvent it, actively work at forgiving and releasing everyone who ever hurt you, and let them stay in the past by creating new potentials for your life today.

Our lives exist in the present and everything that we can do, every wonderful thing that we can create for ourselves, everything that we can want to manifest in our reality, can only happen once we let go of the past.

In the past you have been (and still are) a victim.

You can be a VICTOR in the present moment.

What does being in the present moment mean and how do you get there? The answer to that is very simple and I didn't fully realize what it meant until I wrote an article about it a few years ago. The article was a channeled message for my weekly Enlightening Life newsletter and I wrote it in less than ten minutes, during an inspired moment in which I asked a question and the answer arrived immediately.

The title of the article is 'You Live From One Breath to the Next' and it described how our life exists in the moment we're breathing. You can find a copy on the victimvictorbook.com website No other moment matters when it comes to breath because it is the one thing we cannot live without.

Think about it, a baby takes its first breath the moment it is born and we take our last breath at the moment we die. All during the course of our lives, whether we are awake or asleep, we are breathing and that is what sustains life. If you need a present moment reminder, focus on the next few breaths you take, breathe in and out deeply, and remember that this is the present moment, where you are taking in each life-giving and life-sustaining breath.

As you are creating the life of your dreams and becoming a VICTOR in your life, you will be successful as long as you keep your focus on what is happening right now—not what happened ten or fifteen years ago or even ten or fifteen minutes ago.

Stay focused on what you want to do now, in the present and in this moment, and you will be successful in becoming a VICTOR in your life.

Top Ten VICTOR Tips

1. A VICTOR transforms from the inside out, conquering their internal fears to overcome the paralyzing doubt and confusion that limits their joy.
2. You are re-programming your brain to create new thought habits, so it is important that you remind yourself often that you are a VICTOR.
3. You have to Be, Do and Act to truly incorporate your VICTOR mindset into every part of your life and make it part of who you are. You have to believe in yourself before you can convince others to believe in you.
4. Your beliefs and perceptions are the driving force in your life -- change those and you can change the way you relate to the world and the way the world relates to you, from victim to victor.
5. Stay focused on your goals, intentions, and your dreams. Create a powerful vision for your life, affirm it every day, and replace your victim thinking with victory-focused beliefs, thoughts, and actions.
6. You may lose your old victim friends and gain new ones who appreciate you as a victor because they are victors too.
7. Everything that you want, including the life of your dreams, is available to you when you believe that it is possible because it's already in your field of potential, waiting to connect with you.
8. "As Within, So Without" You mirror your inner self to the world. Whatever you think and believe about yourself is what you project to others and they will respond accordingly.

9. Avoid all negative self-talk, crippling words, and statements. Watch your words and watch your life change.

10. Keep moving forward, every day, day by day. Change will happen as long as you believe that it is possible and you maintain your focus on what you want.

Remember the Universal Law of Attraction--you attract to yourself whatever you think about, talk about and focus on.

Create positive possibilities and you will create the vacuum that will allow your most wonderful possibilities to manifest in your life.

You 'will' something by believing that it is possible and that creates the circumstances for it to be possible. So, get started now. You have waited long enough. Have fun with your new perspective, your new beliefs and your new life. Believe that you deserve the very best that life has to offer and go for it.

I AM A VICTOR!

ABOUT JENNIFER HOFFMAN

Jennifer Hoffman is a globally celebrated Energy Savante, the world's most accurate Intuitive Master, a Best Selling author, speaker, and popular radio show host who helps a global audience raise their vibes, connect to their highest energy potential and greatest level of fulfillment, joy, peace, and prosperity in their lives. Paralyzed by a vaccine when she was five years old, Jennifer's miraculous return to full mobility provided her with powerful lessons in determination, overcoming defeat, overcoming victim based thinking, and succeeding against impossible odds, that have become the foundation in her work of sharing messages of and methods for empowered, energized, self-aware, determined, purpose-filled, masterful living to a global audience.

Through her coaching, programs, books and workshops, including the High Vibes Living® and Core 4 Healing to Wholeness™ programs, Jennifer offers a wealth of information to help others learn how to rise from their paralyzing fear and crippling thoughts and beliefs and dream big, achieving their highest potential to know joy, peace, love, and prosperity in every aspect of their lives.

She is the author of the weekly Enlightening Life newsletter, published on-line since 2004, with more than 4 million readers and several books, including the highly acclaimed *Ascending into Miracles – the Path of Spiritual Mastery* and *30 Days to Everyday Miracles*. Jennifer's ground breaking expose of mind and energy control technologies used by governments and agencies around the world to control human energy has garnered critical acclaim for her book *The Human Energy Control Protocols*.

Through her weekly Enlightening Life radio show, a Blog Talk Radio top performer since 2008 Jennifer connects with millions as she delivers messages that are a source of inspiration and transformation to her loyal listener base.

As one of the world's most accurate intuitive advisors, an expert at energy alignment, intention, congruence, alchemy, and transformation, a respected spiritual teacher and mentor, and Jennifer is celebrated for providing accurate, soul baring guidance, so her clients can choose to live in energetic congruence, intentionally, purposefully, masterfully, and authentically aligned with their highest vision and purpose for their life.

An accomplished and savvy business owner with decades of business experience, Jennifer combines sound business processes, professional expertise, intuitive insights, and leading edge technical knowledge in her business startup and coaching programs, part of the GPS Business Systems division.

With more than twenty years of corporate experience and multiple business degrees, she is the world's most qualified and experienced business trainer and advisor. Her focus is on process, promotion, profits, and productivity, for entrepreneurs and business owners who want to start a scalable business, increase current business revenues, streamline processes, connect and communicate effectively with customers, create new revenue streams, and manage a business efficiently, proactively, productively, and profitably.

Jennifer teaches live and on-line workshops, seminars, keynotes and also offers group and private coaching and training. Connect with Jennifer and information about her products and programs is available at enlighteninglife.com.

www.ingramcontent.com/pod-product-compliance
Lightning Source LLC
LaVergne TN
LVHW022317080426
835509LV00036B/2174
9780982194959